SHURLEY ENGLISH

HOMESCHOOL MADE EASY

LEVEL 1

Student Book

By

Brenda Shurley

Shurley Instructional Materials, Inc., Cabot, Arkansas

04-11
ISBN 978-1-58561-049-5 (Level 1 Student Workbook)

Printed in the United States of America by RR Donnelley, Owensville, MO.

For additional information or to place an order, write to: Shurley Instructional Materials, Inc.
366 SIM Drive
Cabot, AR 72023

1 2 3 4 5 6   11 09 07 05 03 02

JINGLE

SECTION

Jingle Section

Jingle 1: Noun Jingle

This little noun
Floating around
Names a person, place, or thing.
With a knick knack, paddy wack,
These are English rules.
Isn't language fun and cool?

Jingle 2: Verb Jingle

A verb shows action,
There's no doubt!
It tells what the
subject does,
Like sing and shout.

Action verbs are fun to do.
Now, it's time to name a few.
So, clap your hands
And join our rhyme;
Say those verbs
In record time!

Wiggle, jiggle, turn around;
Raise your arms
And stomp the ground.
Shake your finger
And wink your eye;
Wave those action verbs
good-bye.

Jingle 3: Sentence Jingle

A sentence, sentence, sentence
Is complete, complete, complete
When 5 simple rules
It meets, meets, meets.

It has a subject, subject, subject
And a verb, verb, verb.
It makes sense, sense, sense
With every word, word, word.

Add a capital letter, letter
And an end mark, mark.
Now, we're finished, and aren't we smart!
Now, our sentence has all its parts!

REMEMBER
Subject, Verb, Com-plete sense,
Capital letter, and an end mark, too.
That's what a sentence is all about!

Jingle Section

Jingle 4: Adverb Jingle

An adverb modifies a verb.
An adverb asks *How? When? Where?*
To find an adverb: **Go, Ask, Get**.
Where do I **go**? To a verb.
What do I **ask**? How? When? Where?
What do I **get**? An ADVERB! (Clap) (Clap) That's what!

Jingle 5: Adjective Jingle

An adjective modifies a noun.
An adjective asks *What kind? Which one? How many?*
To find an adjective: **Go, Ask, Get**.
Where do I **go**? To a noun.
What do I **ask**? What kind? Which one? How many?
What do I **get**? An ADJECTIVE! (Clap) (Clap) That's what!

Jingle 6: Article Adjective Jingle

We are the article adjectives,
Teeny, tiny adjectives:
A, AN, THE - A, AN, THE.

We are called article adjectives and noun markers;
We are memorized and used every day.
So, if you spot us, you can mark us
With the label A.

We are the article adjectives,
Teeny, tiny adjectives:
A, AN, THE - A, AN, THE.

Jingle Section

Jingle 7: Preposition Jingle

A PREP PREP PREPOSITION
Is a special group of words
That connects a
NOUN, NOUN, NOUN
Or a PRO, PRO, PRONOUN
To the rest of the sentence.

Jingle 8: Object of the Prep Jingle

Dum De Dum Dum!
An O-P is a N-O-U-N or a P-R-O
After the P-R-E-P
In a S-E-N-T-E-N-C-E.
Dum De Dum Dum - DONE!

VOCABULARY

SECTION

VOCABULARY TIME – LEVEL 1

Chapter 6, Vocabulary Words #1	Chapter 6, Vocabulary Words #2
cats, boys, bears, sat, ran	girls, dogs, played

Chapter 6, Vocabulary Words #3	Chapter 6, Vocabulary Words #4
walked, airplanes, flew	ducks, barked, kittens

Chapter 7, Vocabulary Words #1	Chapter 7, Vocabulary Words #2
quietly, today, fast	quickly, loudly, slowly

Chapter 7, Vocabulary Words #3	Chapter 7, Vocabulary Words #4
swiftly, yesterday, low	away, jumped, puppies

Chapter 8, Vocabulary Words #1	Chapter 8, Vocabulary Words #2
two, black, big, brown	three, laughed, squirmy

Chapter 8, Vocabulary Words #3	Chapter 8, Vocabulary Words #4
several, little, happily, four	yellow, waddled, children

Chapter 9, Vocabulary Words #1	Chapter 9, Vocabulary Words #2
yawned, horse, raced	excited, shouted, tired

Chapter 9, Vocabulary Words #3	Chapter 9, Vocabulary Words #4
large, ships, sailed, rapidly	busy, beavers, worked

Chapter 10, Vocabulary Words #1	Chapter 10, Vocabulary Words #2
stopped, suddenly, clowns	five, home, cute, baby

Chapter 10, Vocabulary Words #3	Chapter 10, Vocabulary Words #4
unhappy, cried, happy, six	hungry, birds, monkeys

Chapter 11, Vocabulary Words #1	Chapter 11, Vocabulary Words #2
silly, around, beautiful, car	weary, brothers, ants, crawled, noisily

Chapter 11, Vocabulary Words #3	Chapter 11, Vocabulary Words #4
students, hard, lazy, green, frog	funny, shy, fox, thin

Vocabulary – Level 1 (continued)

Chapter 12, Vocabulary Words #1	Chapter 12, Vocabulary Words #2
tiger, seven, balloon, floated	giant, slept, soundly, hopped

Chapter 12, Vocabulary Words #3	Chapter 12, Vocabulary Words #4
jets, landed, frightened, ate	red, flowers, grew, pretty

Chapter 13, Vocabulary Words #1	Chapter 13, Vocabulary Words #2
house, smoothly, runway, shade, (to, on, in)	bee, softly, poor, fell, mud, (by)

Chapter 13, Vocabulary Words #3	Chapter 13, Vocabulary Words #4
huge, snake, road, tiny, (across, at)	friends, movies, dime, door

Chapter 14, Vocabulary Words #1	Chapter 14, Vocabulary Words #2
jelly, jar, floor, lake	music, store, camped, mountains

Chapter 14, Vocabulary Words #3	Chapter 14, Vocabulary Words #4
rabbit, rain, waited, bus	window, waved, passengers, looked, bananas

Chapter 15, Vocabulary Words #1	Chapter 15, Vocabulary Words #2
grasshopper, garden, deer, swans	family, beach, crib, eight, small

Chapter 15, Vocabulary Words #3	Chapter 15, Vocabulary Words #4
church, old, gray, white, (down)	shivering, whimpered, ocean, crashed, rocks

Chapter 16, Vocabulary Words #1	Chapter 16, Vocabulary Words #2
kites, high, sky	nine, silently, rolled

Chapter 16, Vocabulary Words #3	Chapter 16, Vocabulary Words #4
pony, trotted, pink, pig	bell, rang, valley, sailor, map

Chapter 17, Vocabulary Words #1	Chapter 17, Vocabulary Words #2
rode, train, went, zoo	sun, city, opened, early, pond

Chapter 17, Vocabulary Words #3	Chapter 17, Vocabulary Words #4
library, book, carefully, ice	volcano, erupted, ten, swam

Chapter 18, Vocabulary Words #1	Chapter 18, Vocabulary Words #2
Tim, street, otters, water, salty, popcorn	clever, field, new, sleds, hill

Chapter 18, Vocabulary Words #3	Chapter 18, Vocabulary Words #4
snow, shines, brightly, gate	barn, mouse, James

Vocabulary – Level 1 (continued)

Chapter 19, Vocabulary Words #1	Chapter 19, Vocabulary Words #2
log, wagon, scampered	Anna, fog, tall, Sam

Chapter 19, Vocabulary Words #3	Chapter 19, Vocabulary Words #4
gathered, roses, circus, pranced, proudly	kind, nurse, patient

Chapter 20, Vocabulary Words #1	Chapter 20, Vocabulary Words #2
excitedly, boat, fireflies, glowed, dark	animals, tree, mall

Chapter 20, Vocabulary Words #3	Chapter 20, Vocabulary Words #4
neighborhood, airport, strong, fished, stream	purple, summer, blue, blew

Chapter 21, Vocabulary Words #1	Chapter 21, Vocabulary Words #2
orange, socks	fireman, climbed, roof, butterfly, Dan

Chapter 21, Vocabulary Words #3	Chapter 21, Vocabulary Words #4
candles, burned, lost	Sarah, dressed, warmly, winter

Chapter 22, Vocabulary Words #1	Chapter 22, Vocabulary Words #2
ground, melted, goats, stood, porch	birthday, cake, pool

Chapter 22, Vocabulary Words #3	Chapter 22, Vocabulary Words #4
best, coins, path	hall, Mom, shopped, park

Chapter 23, Vocabulary Words #1	Chapter 23, Vocabulary Words #2
donkeys, geese	sand, truck, turned, pumpkins

Chapter 23, Vocabulary Words #3	Chapter 23, Vocabulary Words #4
young, smiled, spider	eggs, hatched, cheerfully, school

Chapter 24, Vocabulary Words #1	Chapter 24, Vocabulary Words #2
Grandmother, mailbox, together	bloomed, trail, camel, desert

Chapter 24, Vocabulary Words #3	Chapter 24, Vocabulary Words #4
eagle, gracefully, bouncy, grandchildren	raccoons, soldiers, marched, parade

Chapter 25, Vocabulary Words #1	Chapter 25, Vocabulary Words #2
stray, teacher, kindly	sisters, smoke, drifted, stared, hungrily, honey

Chapter 25, Vocabulary Words #3	Chapter 25, Vocabulary Words #4
bubbles, distant, twinkled, thick	angry, buzzed, overhead, beetle

SYNONYM AND ANTONYM

SECTION

SYNONYM AND ANTONYM TIME – LEVEL 1

Chapter 7: Underline the **syn** if the words are synonyms. Underline the **ant** if the words are antonyms.

1. in, out	syn	ant	2. right, wrong	syn	ant	3. quit, stop	syn	ant

Chapter 8: Underline the **syn** if the words are synonyms. Underline the **ant** if the words are antonyms.

1. over, under	syn	ant	2. warm, cold	syn	ant	3. stone, rock	syn	ant

Chapter 9: Underline the **syn** if the words are synonyms. Underline the **ant** if the words are antonyms.

1. up, down	syn	ant	2. push, pull	syn	ant	3. start, begin	syn	ant

Chapter 10: Underline the **syn** if the words are synonyms. Underline the **ant** if the words are antonyms.

1. giant, huge	syn	ant	2. front, back	syn	ant	3. rough, smooth	syn	ant

Chapter 11: Underline the **syn** if the words are synonyms. Underline the **ant** if the words are antonyms.

1. form, shape	syn	ant	2. inside, outside	syn	ant	3. end, finish	syn	ant

Chapter 12: Underline the **syn** if the words are synonyms. Underline the **ant** if the words are antonyms.

1. high, low	syn	ant	2. open, close	syn	ant	3. tiny, small	syn	ant

Chapter 13: Underline the **syn** if the words are synonyms. Underline the **ant** if the words are antonyms.

1. far, near	syn	ant	2. rush, hurry	syn	ant	3. part, piece	syn	ant

Chapter 14: Underline the **syn** if the words are synonyms. Underline the **ant** if the words are antonyms.

1. above, below	syn	ant	2. old, new	syn	ant	3. lean, thin	syn	ant

Chapter 15: Underline the **syn** if the words are synonyms. Underline the **ant** if the words are antonyms.

1. left, right	syn	ant	2. poor, rich	syn	ant	3. puzzle, riddle	syn	ant

Synonym and Antonym – Level 1 (continued)

Chapter 16: Underline the **syn** if the words are synonyms. Underline the **ant** if the words are antonyms.

1. on, off	syn ant	2. tall, short	syn ant	3. kind, good	syn ant

Chapter 17: Underline the **syn** if the words are synonyms. Underline the **ant** if the words are antonyms.

1. top, bottom	syn ant	2. hard, firm	syn ant	3. evil, bad	syn ant

Chapter 18: Underline the **syn** if the words are synonyms. Underline the **ant** if the words are antonyms.

1. before, after	syn ant	2. lost, found	syn ant	3. sick, ill	syn ant

Chapter 19: Underline the **syn** if the words are synonyms. Underline the **ant** if the words are antonyms.

1. front, back	syn ant	2. early, late	syn ant	3. simple, easy	syn ant

Chapter 20: Underline the **syn** if the words are synonyms. Underline the **ant** if the words are antonyms.

1. first, last	syn ant	2. slow, quick	syn ant	3. raise, lift	syn ant

Chapter 21: Underline the **syn** if the words are synonyms. Underline the **ant** if the words are antonyms.

1. sweet, sour	syn ant	2. below, beneath	syn ant	3. aid, help	syn ant

Chapter 22: Underline the **syn** if the words are synonyms. Underline the **ant** if the words are antonyms.

1. night, day	syn ant	2. shout, whisper	syn ant	3. bashful, shy	syn ant

Chapter 23: Underline the **syn** if the words are synonyms. Underline the **ant** if the words are antonyms.

1. sell, buy	syn ant	2. ask, tell	syn ant	3. calm, quiet	syn ant

Chapter 24: Underline the **syn** if the words are synonyms. Underline the **ant** if the words are antonyms.

1. wild, tame	syn ant	2. add, subtract	syn ant	3. push, shove	syn ant

Chapter 25: Underline the **syn** if the words are synonyms. Underline the **ant** if the words are antonyms.

1. bright, dim	syn ant	2. round, square	syn ant	3. pull, tug	syn ant

Notes

REFERENCE

SECTION

Reference 1: Three Rules of a SENTENCE

1. The WORDS tell who or what the SENTENCE is about.
2. The WORDS tell what something does.
3. The WORDS should make complete sense.

Reference 2: What is Journal Writing?

Journal Writing is a written record of your personal thoughts and feelings about things or people that are important to you. You can record your dreams, memories, feelings, and experiences. You can ask questions and answer some of them. It is fun to go back later and read what you have written because it shows how you have changed in different areas of your life. Writing in a journal is an easy and enjoyable way to practice your writing skills without worrying about a writing grade.

What do I write about?

Journals are personal, but sometimes it helps to have ideas to get you started. Remember, in a journal, you do not have to stick to one topic. Write about someone or something you like. Write about what you did last weekend or on vacation. Write about what you hope to do this week or on your next vacation. Write about home, school, friends, hobbies, special talents (yours or someone else's), or the hopes and fears you have about things now and in the future. If something bothers you, record it in your journal. If something interests you, record it. After all, it is your journal!

How do I get started writing in my personal journal?

You need to put the day's date on the title line of your paper: **Month, Day, Year.** Skip the next line and begin your entry. You might write one or two sentences, a paragraph, a whole page, or several pages. Except for the journal date, no particular organizational style is required for journal writing. You decide how best to organize and express your thoughts. Feel free to include pictures or lists if they will help you remember your thoughts about different things. You will also need a spiral notebook, a pen, a quiet place, and at least 5-10 minutes of uninterrupted writing time.

Note: Any drawings you might include do not have to be masterpieces — stick figures will do nicely.

Reference 3: Synonyms and Antonyms

Definitions: Synonyms are words that have similar, or almost the same, meanings.
Antonyms are words that have opposite, or different, meanings.

Directions: Identify each pair of words as synonyms or antonyms by drawing a line under the *syn* or *ant*.

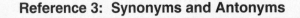

1. small, tiny   <u>syn</u>   ant   2. up, down   syn   <u>ant</u>   3. happy, cheerful   <u>syn</u>   ant

Reference 4: Definitions for Complete Subject, Complete Predicate

1. The **complete subject** is the subject and all the words that describe the subject.
2. The **complete predicate** is the verb and all the words that describe the verb.

Sample Sentence: The little brown pony galloped swiftly yesterday.

Reference 5: Two Kinds of Sentences

1. A **statement** is a sentence that <u>tells</u> something. A statement starts with a capital letter and ends with a <u>period</u>. Example: **T**he big bear walked away**.**	2. A **question** is a sentence that <u>asks</u> something. A question starts with a capital letter and ends with a <u>question mark</u>. Example: **D**o the boys work here**?**

Reference 6: Parts-of-Speech Word Bank

On notebook paper, write a sentence using the words in the Word Bank. Put the words you select in the same order as the Sentence Labels listed below. Write the correct label above each word in your sentence.

Nouns	Verbs	Adjectives	Adverbs
puppies kittens duck	barked, quacked, yawned, climbed, played, waddled, ran	a, an, the, two, black, yellow, brown, excited, sleepy, hungry, unhappy, cute, little	loudly, excitedly, fast, happily, rapidly, noisily, quietly, today

Sentence Labels: A Adj SN V Adv   or   A Adj Adj SN V Adv Adv

Sentence Examples:

1. The sleepy puppies yawned noisily.   2. The two excited puppies barked loudly today.

Sentence Checklist:

1. Did you follow the labels?   3. Did you check for the five sentence parts?
2. Did you use the words in the Word Bank?   4. Did you write neatly?

Reference 7: A and An Choices

Rule 1: Use the word **a** when the next word begins with a consonant sound. (*Example: a tree*)
Rule 2: Use the word **an** when the next word begins with a vowel sound. (*Example: an orange*)

Sample Sentences: Write **a** or **an** in the blanks.

1. David saw __**an**__ old eagle.

2. David saw __**a**__ young eagle.

3. The chef baked __**a**__ pie.

4. The chef baked __**an**__ apple pie.

Reference 8: Preposition and Object of the Preposition

SN V P A OP
Sam fell down the hill.

In the sample sentence, *Sam fell **down the hill***, the word *down* is a preposition because it has the noun *hill* after it that answers the question **what**. To find the preposition and object of the preposition in the Question and Answer Flow, say:

down - Preposition
down what? hill - Object of the Preposition

Reference 9: Parts-of-Speech Word Bank With Prepositional Phrases

On notebook paper, write a sentence using the words in the Word Bank. Put the words you select in the same order as the Sentence Labels listed below. Write the correct label above each word in your sentence.

WORD BANK

Nouns	Verbs	Adjectives	Adverbs	Prepositional Phrases
children dogs otters	swam splashed played	a, an, the, four, several, young, brown, happy, excited	gracefully, playfully, joyfully, happily, merrily, loudly	in the water on the beach by the trees

Sentence Labels: A Adj SN V Adv Prep Phrase   or   Adj SN V Adv Prep Phrase

Examples:

1. Several children played merrily on the beach.

2. Four otters swam playfully in the water.

3. The young dogs splashed loudly in the water.

4. The brown dogs played happily by the trees.

5. The excited children splashed loudly in the water.

6. Several otters swam gracefully by the trees.

Reference 10: Knowing the Difference Between Prepositions and Adverbs

In the sample sentence, *Sam fell **down***, the word *down* is an adverb because it tells where and does not have a noun after it.

In the sample sentence, *Sam fell **down the hill***, the word *down* is a preposition because it has the noun *hill* after it that answers the question **what**. To find the preposition and object of the preposition in the Question and Answer Flow, say:

down - Preposition
down what? hill - Object of the Preposition

Reference 11: Capitalization Rules

1. Capitalize the first word of a sentence.	5. Capitalize the months of the year. (*March, April*)
2. Capitalize the pronoun I.	6. Capitalize the names of cities. (*Dallas*)
3. Capitalize the names of people. (*Kelly, Billy*)	7. Capitalize the names of states. (*Missouri*)
4. Capitalize the days of the week. (*Monday, Tuesday*)	

Examples

Directions: Correct each capitalization mistake and write the rule number above the corrections. Put a (.) or a (?) at the end of each sentence.

___1_____(capitalization rule numbers) **T** 1. the big dog barked loudly _._ **(1 capital)**	_1 (or 2)_____4_____5_____(capitalization rule numbers) **I** **F** **J** 4. i worked one friday in june _._ **(3 capitals)**
___1___2_____(capitalization rule numbers) **M** **I** 2. may i play here _?_ **(2 capitals)**	___1_____3_____6_____7 (capitalization rule numbers) **W** **J** **O** **F** 5. we talked to jim in orlando, florida _._ **(4 capitals)**
___1_____3____(capitalization rule numbers) **H** **T** 3. he ran to tommy _._ **(2 capitals)**	

Reference 12: Definitions for Singular and Plural Nouns

1. A **singular noun** usually does not end in *s* or *es* and means only one. (*ship, clown, cat*)
   <u>Exception</u>: Some nouns that end in s are singular and mean only one. (*glass, mess, class*)
2. A **plural noun** usually ends in *s* or *es* and means more than one. (*ships, clowns, cats*)
   <u>Exception</u>: Some nouns are made plural by changing their spelling. (*tooth - teeth, woman - women*)

Reference 13: Singular and Plural Nouns

For each noun listed below, write **S** for singular or **P** for plural.

Noun	S or P	Noun	S or P	Noun	S or P
1. trees	P	4. child	S	7. shoes	P
2. tooth	S	5. teeth	P	8. children	P
3. frog	S	6. bus	S	9. tiger	S

Reference 14: Definitions for Common and Proper Nouns

1. A **common noun** names ANY person, place, or thing. A common noun is not capitalized because it does not name a specific person, place, or thing. (*trees, lake*)

2. A **proper noun** is a noun that names a specific, or particular, person, place, or thing. Proper nouns are always capitalized no matter where they are located in the sentence. (*Matthew, Hawaii*)

Reference 15: Common and Proper Nouns

For each noun listed below, write **C** for common or **P** for proper.

Noun	C or P	Noun	C or P	Noun	C or P
1. Christmas	P	4. Texas	P	7. Denver	P
2. jar	C	5. Sam	P	8. coat	C
3. nurse	C	6. horse	C	9. girl	C

Reference 16: Sample Vocabulary Words for Practice and Improved Sentences

Nouns		Verbs	Adjectives	Adverbs	Prepositions
boys	girls	laughed	a, an, the	quietly	across
brother	sailor	raced	hungry	quickly	at
cars	ship	walked	red	happily	down
horse	bears	sat	three	today	in
mother	father	jumped	friendly	loudly	on
monkeys	bees	sailed	angry	slowly	to
cats	dogs	climbed	happy	noisily	by
students	airplane	flew	sleepy	yesterday	

Reference 17: The Topic		
Finding the topic: Write the name of the topic that best describes what each column of words is about. Choose from these topics: **Trees Colors Animals Books Holidays**.		
(1) **Animals**	(2) **Holidays**	(3) **Colors**
squirrel	Thanksgiving	purple
raccoon	Easter	black
rabbit	Christmas	yellow

Reference 18: Supporting and Non-Supporting Ideas		
Words and ideas that support the topic: In each column, cross out the one word or idea that does not support the underlined topic at the top.		
(1) **Zoo Animals**	(2) **Fruit**	(3) **Numbers**
monkey	apple	four
elephant	banana	~~jelly~~
tiger	~~wheat~~	nine
~~umbrella~~	peach	seven

Reference 19: Supporting and Non-Supporting Sentences
Sentences that support the topic: Read each topic. Then, cross out the one sentence that does not support the topic.
Topic: My New Tree House 1. My dad built a tree house for my birthday. 2. My tree house is way up in an oak tree. 3. ~~My dad gave me a bat for Christmas.~~ 4. My friends come over, and we play in my new tree house.

Reference 20: Two-Point Expository Paragraph Example

List of colors: red, blue, green, yellow, white, orange, brown, black, pink, gray, and purple.

Topic: **My Favorite colors**
Two main points: 1. **orange**   2. **green**

Sentence #1 – <u>Topic Sentence</u> (*Use words in the topic and tell how many points will be used.*)
I have two favorite colors.

Sentence #2 – <u>Two-Point Sentence</u> (*List the 2 points in the order you will present them.*)
These colors are orange and green.

Sentence #3 – <u>First Point</u>
My first favorite color is orange.

Sentence #4 – <u>Supporting Sentence</u> for the first point.
I like orange because my pet goldfish is a bright shade of orange.

Sentence #5 – <u>Second Point</u>
My second favorite color is green.

Sentence #6 – <u>Supporting Sentence</u> for the second point.
Green makes me think of grass, leaves, and going outside to play in the summertime.

Sentence #7 – <u>Concluding (final) Sentence</u>. (*Restate the topic sentence and add an extra thought.*)
My two favorite colors make me happy because they remind me of fun things.

SAMPLE PARAGRAPH   **My Favorite Colors**

   I have two favorite colors. These colors are orange and green. My first favorite color is orange. I like orange because my pet goldfish is a bright shade of orange. My second favorite color is green. Green makes me think of grass, leaves, and going outside to play in the summertime. My two favorite colors make me happy because they remind me of fun things.

General Checklist: Check the Finished Paragraph	The Two-Point Expository Paragraph Outline
(1) Have you followed the pattern for a two-point paragraph? (*Indent, topic sentence, 2-point sentence, 2 main points, 2 supporting sentences, and a concluding sentence.*) (2) Do you have complete sentences? (3) Have you capitalized the first word and put an end mark at the end of every sentence? (4) Have you checked your sentences for capitalization and end-mark mistakes?	Topic 2 points about the topic Sentence #1: **Topic** sentence Sentence #2: A **two-point** sentence Sentence #3: A **first-point** sentence Sentence #4: A **supporting** sentence for the first point Sentence #5: A **second-point** sentence Sentence #6: A **supporting** sentence for the second point Sentence #7: A **concluding** sentence

Reference 21: Paragraph for Singular and Plural Points

Two-Point Expository Paragraph

Topic: My favorite animals
2-points: 1. beavers 2. otters

      I have two favorite animals. These animals are beavers and otters. My first favorite animal is a beaver. I think watching beavers build a dam across a river is very fascinating. My second favorite animal is an otter. I like otters because they are so funny when they play in the water. My two favorite animals are fun to watch at work and at play.

Reference 22: Complete Sentences and Sentence Fragments

Identifying complete sentences and sentence fragments: Write **S** for a complete sentence and **F** for a sentence fragment on the line beside each group of words below.

S	1. The fish were swimming around in the aquarium.
F	2. For a few dollars.
S	3. The replacement part arrived yesterday.
S	4. George laughed.
F	5. Played during the recital.
F	6. The peaches on the trees.

Reference 23: Matching Subject Parts and Predicate Parts

Match each subject part with the correct predicate part by writing the correct sentence number in the blank.

1.	The purple crayon	3	climbed to the top of the tree.
2.	A white truck	1	broke in half.
3.	Two black cats	4	hurt my eyes.
4.	The bright light	2	parked in front of the store.

Reference 24: Contractions

isn't is not	aren't are not	wasn't was not	weren't were not
The pen **is not** here.	The books **are not** new.	The cat **was not** outside.	The boys **were not** early.
The pen **isn't** here.	The books **aren't** new.	The cat **wasn't** outside.	The boys **weren't** early.

Reference 25: More Contractions				
I'm **I am**	**can't** **cannot**	**don't** **do not**	**doesn't** **does not**	**didn't** **did not**
I am not home.	You **cannot** go.	We **do not** see you.	The man **does not** hear.	I **did not** know.
I'm not home.	You **can't** go.	We **don't** see you.	The man **doesn't** hear.	I **didn't** know.

Reference 26: Present, Past, and Future Verb Tenses

When you are writing paragraphs, you must use verbs that are in the same tense. **Tense** means time. The tense of a verb shows the time of the action. There are three basic tenses that show when an action takes place. They are **past tense, present tense,** and **future tense.** Now, you will learn to recognize each kind of tense.

1. The **past tense** shows that something has happened sometime in the past. Most past tense verbs are made past tense by adding an **-ed** to the end of the word. If a verb uses **-ed** to make the past tense form, it is called a **regular** past tense verb: listen-**listened**, talk-**talked**, play-**played**, jump-**jumped**.

   Other past tense verbs are made past tense by changing their **spelling form** and not by adding **-ed**. If a verb uses a spelling change to make the past tense form, it is called an **irregular** past tense verb: give-**gave**, take-**took**, sell-**sold**, buy-**bought**. *(The verbs are listed as regular or irregular for you.)*

2. The **present tense** shows that something is happening now, in the present. Present tense verbs can end with an **–s** for singular subjects or without an **–s** for plural subjects: **listens-listen, talks-talk, plays-play, jumps-jump, gives-give, takes-take, sells-sell, buys-buy.** *(The verbs are listed as regular or irregular for you.)*

3. The **future tense** shows that something will happen at some time in the future. The future tense form always has the helping verb *will* before the main verb. Future tense verb examples: **will talk, will listen, will play, will jump, will see, will give, will take, will sell, will buy.**

Example: Identify the tense of each underlined verb by writing a number **1** for past tense, a number **2** for present tense, or a number **3** for future tense.

Verb Tense	Regular Verbs	Verb Tense	Irregular Verbs
1	1. She listened to the radio.	2	4. Larry sells used cars.
2	2. She listens to the radio.	1	5. Larry sold used cars.
3	3. She will listen to the radio.	3	6. Larry will sell used cars.

Reference 27: Tips for Writing Friendly Letters

Tip #1: Write as if you were talking to the person face-to-face. Share information about yourself and mutual friends. Tell stories, conversations, or jokes. Share pictures, articles, drawings, poems, etc. Avoid saying something about someone else that you'll be sorry for later.

Tip #2: If you are writing a return letter, be sure to answer any questions that were asked. Repeat the question so that your reader will know what you are writing about. (You asked about . . .)

Tip #3: End your letter in a positive way so that your reader will want to write a return letter.

Reference 28: Friendly Letter Example

1. Heading

Write your address.
Write the date.

23 Circle Drive
Dallas, TX 93312
April 3, 20____

2. Friendly Greeting

Name the person receiving the letter.
Use a comma.

Dear Jonathan,

3. Body (Indent Paragraphs)

Write what you want to say. Indent.

Are you playing baseball again this year? I would really like to come to watch one of your games. Please let me know when your season begins.

4. Closing

Capitalize the first word.
Use a comma.

Your cousin,

5. Signature

Sign your name.

Timothy

Reference 29: Thank-You Note for a Gift

What -   Thank you for...
                (tell color, kind, and item)
Use -   Tell how the gift is used.
Thanks - I appreciate your thinking of me at this time.

Example 1: Gift

Heading
3132 Apple Street
Greenwood, KS 15023
June 3, 20____

Greeting
Dear Mrs. Smith,

Body
    Thank you for the book about sea animals. It has been a wonderful research tool for my science project. Thank you for your kindness.

Closing
Sincerely,

Signature
Elizabeth

Reference 30: Thank-You Note for an Action

What -   Thank you for...
                (tell action)
Use -   Tell how the action helped.
Thanks - I appreciate your remembering me.

Example 2: Action

Heading
239 Bluebird Lane
Charleston, SC 99173
August 1, 20____

Greeting
Dear Linda,

Body
    Thank you for visiting me in the hospital. I was so thrilled to see a familiar face. I appreciate your kindness.

Closing
Your friend,

Signature
Kathleen

Reference 31: Alphabetical Order

Directions: Put each group of words in alphabetical order. Use numbers to show the order in each column.

Animal Words	"G" Words	Farm Words	Color Words	"L" Words
2 1. rabbit	**2** 3. garden	**1** 5. barn	**1** 7. black	**2** 9. light
1 2. donkey	**1** 4. game	**2** 6. tractor	**2** 8. blue	**1** 10. leg

Reference 32: Three Main Parts of the Library

<u>Fiction Section</u>
Fiction books contain stories about people, places, or things that are not true.

<u>Nonfiction Section</u>
Nonfiction books contain information and stories that are true.

<u>Reference Section</u>
The Reference Section is designed to help you find information on many topics. The most common reference books are the dictionary and the encyclopedia.

Reference 33: "Piggy Under the Fence"

In the barnyard lived a cute little pig named Piggy. Piggy loved to crawl under the fence. Piggy said, "Under, under, under. Under the fence. My! My! My! I LOVE to crawl under the fence!"

First, the farmer caught Piggy crawling under the fence. The farmer said, "Under, under, under. Under the fence. My! My! My! Piggy LOVES to crawl under the fence! I do not know what to do."

Next, the farmer's wife caught Piggy crawling under the fence. The farmer's wife said, "Under, under, under. Under the fence. My! My! My! Piggy LOVES to crawl under the fence! I do not know what to do."

Then, the farmer's children caught Piggy crawling under the fence. The farmer's children said, "Under, under, under. Under the fence. My! My! My! Piggy LOVES to crawl under the fence! We do not know what to do."

But Piggy's mother did not smile. Piggy's mother said, "Under, under, under. Under the fence. My! My! My! I know what to do. If Piggy crawls under the fence again, Piggy will go over my knee!"

Piggy looked at the fence. Piggy looked at his mother. Then, Piggy said, "Under, under, under. Under the fence. My! My! My! I do NOT like to crawl under the fence anymore!"

Notes

PRACTICE

SECTION

Chapter 10, Lesson 1, Practice: Classify the sentence below. Use **SN** for subject noun, **V** for verb, **Adv** for adverb, **Adj** for adjective, and **A** for article adjective. Underline the complete subject <u>one</u> time and the complete predicate <u>two</u> times.

A	Adj	Adj	SN	V	Adv	Adv
The	seven	white	rabbits	hopped	quickly	away.

Chapter 10, Lesson 2, Practice: Classify the sentence below. Use **SN** for subject noun, **V** for verb, **Adv** for adverb, **Adj** for adjective, and **A** for article adjective. Underline the complete subject <u>one</u> time and the complete predicate <u>two</u> times.

The   three   young   actors   bowed   gracefully.

Chapter 10, Lesson 3, Practice: Classify the sentence below. Use **SN** for subject noun, **V** for verb, **Adv** for adverb, **Adj** for adjective, and **A** for article adjective. Underline the complete subject <u>one</u> time and the complete predicate <u>two</u> times.

The   two   busy   children   played   happily   today.

Chapter 11, Lesson 1, Practice 1: On notebook paper, write each sentence correctly. Capitalize the first word of each sentence and put a (.) or a (?) at the end.

1. did the car lights dim suddenly

2. the chocolate cake baked slowly.

3. the hungry baby cried softly.

4. the school telephone rang loudly.

*The two upset

Chapter 11, Lesson 1, Practice 2: On notebook paper, write a sentence using the words in the Word Bank. Put the words you select in the same order as the Sentence Labels listed below. Write the correct label above each word in your sentence.

WORD BANK			
Nouns	**Verbs**	**Adjectives**	**Adverbs**
babies puppies toddlers	whined, cried, yawned, played, smiled, crawled, napped	a, an, the, two, tiny, upset, hungry, excited, three, pretty, unhappy, sleepy	swiftly, softly, loudly, quietly, happily, noisily, yesterday

Sentence Labels: A Adj SN V Adv (Bonus) A Adj Adj SN V Adv Adv

*The two upset babies whined loudly

Chapter 11, Lesson 2, Practice 1: On notebook paper, write each sentence correctly. Capitalize the first word of each sentence and put a (.) or a (?) at the end.

1. an orange ball bounced slowly

2. was the sun shining brightly

3. the bananas ripened quickly

4. the bees buzzed wildly

Chapter 11, Lesson 2, Practice 2: On notebook paper, write a sentence using the words in the Word Bank. Put the words you select in the same order as the Sentence Labels listed below. Write the correct label above each word in your sentence.

WORD BANK			
Nouns	**Verbs**	**Adjectives**	**Adverbs**
bats sparrows owls	dove, swooped, flew, landed	a, an, the, three, swift, hungry, old, young, brown, black	carelessly dangerously low, high, today

Sentence Labels: A Adj SN V Adv (Bonus) A Adj Adj SN V Adv Adv

Chapter 11, Lesson 3, Practice 1: On notebook paper, write each sentence correctly. Capitalize the first word of each sentence and put a (.) or a (?) at the end.

1. the excited fans cheered loudly

2. did the glass window crack yesterday

3. do bankers work tomorrow

4. the wheat bread baked slowly

Chapter 11, Lesson 3, Practice 2: On notebook paper, write a sentence using the words in the Word Bank. Put the words you select in the same order as the Sentence Labels listed below. Write the correct label above each word in your sentence.

WORD BANK			
Nouns	**Verbs**	**Adjectives**	**Adverbs**
flowers, buds, grass, trees	bloomed, opened, grew, wilted	a, an, the, four, colorful, bright, new, green, yellow, red, large	quickly, rapidly, slowly, today, beautifully, yesterday

Sentence Labels:	A	Adj	Adj	SN	V	Adv	Adv

Chapter 12, Lesson 1, Practice 1: Write *a* or *an* in the blanks.

1. _____ awful storm frightened me.

2. Columbus was _____ explorer.

3. The workers dug _____ hole.

4. Jim found _____ empty can.

5. _____ alarm

6. _____ scarf

7. _____ case

8. _____ acorn

Chapter 12, Lesson 1, Practice 2: On notebook paper, write a sentence using the words in the Word Bank. Put the words you select in the same order as the Sentence Labels listed below. Write the correct label above each word in your sentence.

WORD BANK			
Nouns	**Verbs**	**Adjectives**	**Adverbs**
birds rabbits grasshoppers	hopped, jumped, sat, nibbled, played, hid	a, an, the, cute, three, baby, brown, green, white, gentle, funny, small, shy	merrily, quietly, excitedly, noisily, yesterday, swiftly, slowly, rapidly

Sentence Labels: A Adj SN V Adv (Bonus) A Adj Adj SN V Adv Adv

---

Chapter 12, Lesson 2, Practice 1: Write *a* or *an* in the blanks.

1. The king built _____ castle.

2. She pointed to _____ exit.

3. Our group had _____ guide.

4. _____ elephant looked at me.

5. _____ inch

6. _____ hat

7. _____ hallway

8. _____ elk

Chapter 12, Lesson 2, Practice 2: On notebook paper, write a sentence using the words in the Word Bank. Put the words you select in the same order as the Sentence Labels listed below. Write the correct label above each word in your sentence.

WORD BANK			
Nouns	**Verbs**	**Adjectives**	**Adverbs**
duck swan eagle	glided, flew, soared, landed, floated, swam, ran, ate	a, an, the, one, white, large, baby, beautiful, brown, strong, brave, loud, small	gracefully, quietly, rapidly, swiftly, high, far, away, gently, today, loudly, softly

Sentence Labels: A Adj SN V Adv (Bonus) A Adj Adj SN V Adv Adv

---

Chapter 12, Lesson 3, Practice 1: Write *a* or *an* in the blanks.

1. A gorilla is _____ animal.

2. The man carried _____ package.

3. Dad bought _____ computer.

4. She bought _____ extra suitcase.

5. _____ apron

6. _____ lemon

7. _____ ruler

8. _____ office

Chapter 12, Lesson 3, Practice 2: On notebook paper, write a sentence using the words in the Word Bank. Put the words you select in the same order as the Sentence Labels listed below. Write the correct label above each word in your sentence.

WORD BANK			
Nouns	**Verbs**	**Adjectives**	**Adverbs**
cows horses goats	grazed, drank, walked, stood, ran, ate, worked, chewed, slept, kicked	a, an, the, two, black, lazy, old, brown, young, small, large, smart, frightened	calmly, excitedly, fast, happily, noisily, quietly, today, daily, soundly, hard

Sentence Labels: A Adj SN V Adv (Bonus) A Adj Adj SN V Adv Adv

---

Chapter 14, Lesson 2, Practice 1: Write *a* or *an* in the blanks.

1. The farmer drove _____ tractor.

2. Pat read _____ adventure story.

3. He drove _____ new car.

4. Sara picked _____ red rose.

5. _____ alligator

6. _____ elbow

7. _____ candle

8. _____ orange

Chapter 14, Lesson 2, Practice 2: On notebook paper, write a sentence using the words in the Word Bank. Put the words you select in the same order as the Sentence Labels listed below. Write the correct label above each word in your sentence.

WORD BANK

Nouns	Verbs	Adjectives	Adverbs	Prepositional Phrases
students children soldiers	talked, chatted, whispered, laughed	a, an, the, four, young, excited, busy, happy, lazy, little, silly, shy, tired	quietly cautiously secretly noisily	on the telephone across the table by the store in the restaurant

Sentence Labels: A Adj Adj SN V Adv Prep Phrase

Chapter 14, Lesson 3, Practice 1: On notebook paper, write a sentence using the words in the Word Bank. Put the words you select in the same order as the Sentence Labels listed below. Write the correct label above each word in your sentence.

WORD BANK

Nouns	Verbs	Adjectives	Adverbs	Prepositional Phrases
mouse squirrel raccoons	jumped moved ran	a, an, the, old, brown, young, three, eager,	loudly, quickly, noisily, silently, slowly, today	down the road across the yard on the porch

Sentence Labels: A Adj Adj SN V Adv Prep Phrase

Chapter 14, Lesson 3, Practice 2: Classify the sentence below. Use **SN** for subject noun, **V** for verb, **Adv** for adverb, **Adj** for adjective, **A** for article adjective, **P** for preposition, and **OP** for object of the preposition. Underline the complete subject <u>one</u> time and the complete predicate <u>two</u> times.

The little yellow ducks swam happily in the pond.

Chapter 15, Lesson 1, Practice: Correct the capitalization mistakes and put the rule number above each correction. Use the rule numbers in Reference 11 on page 17 in the Reference Section of your book. Put a (.) or a (?) at the end of the sentence.

_____ (capitalization rule numbers)

alice   wrote   a   letter   to   julie   on   thursday _____ (3 capitals)

Chapter 15, Lesson 2, Practice: Correct the capitalization mistakes and put the rule number above each correction. Use the rule numbers in Reference 11 on page 17 in the Reference Section of your book. Put a (.) or a (?) at the end of the sentence.

_____ (capitalization rule numbers)

timothy   moved   to   tuscon,   arizona,   last   july _____ (4 capitals)

Chapter 15, Lesson 3, Practice 1: Correct the capitalization mistakes and put the rule number above each correction. Use the rule numbers in Reference 11 on page 17 in the Reference Section of your book. Put a (.) or a (?) at the end of the sentence.

_____(capitalization rule numbers)

1. may   i   visit   mary   on   wednesday _____ (4 capitals)

_____(capitalization rule numbers)

2. chris   lives   in   seattle,   washington _____ (3 capitals)

Chapter 15, Lesson 3, Practice 2: On notebook paper, write a sentence using the words in the Word Bank. Put the words you select in the same order as the Sentence Labels listed below. Write the correct label above each word in your sentence.

WORD BANK

Nouns	Verbs	Adjectives	Adverbs	Prepositional Phrases
wind breeze storm	blew gusted howled	a, an, the, cold, refreshing, hot, severe, spring, soft, gentle, harsh, dark, summer, winter	loudly, strongly, suddenly, today, calmly, silently, yesterday	across the lake at night in the tunnel during the day in the mountains

Sentence Labels: A Adj SN V Adv Prep Phrase

Independent Exercise: Choose your own Sentence Labels.

Chapter 16, Lesson 1, Practice: For each noun listed below, write **S** for singular or **P** for plural.

Noun	S or P	Noun	S or P	Noun	S or P
1. bears		5. ants		9. cars	
2. goose		6. balloon		10. geese	
3. babies		7. feet		11. church	
4. dog		8. foot		12. windows	

Chapter 16, Lesson 2, Practice: For each noun listed below, write **S** for singular or **P** for plural.

Noun	S or P	Noun	S or P	Noun	S or P
1. sleds		5. women		9. turtles	
2. flower		6. horse		10. mice	
3. kittens		7. clowns		11. foxes	
4. mouse		8. crib		12. pig	

Chapter 16, Lesson 3, Practice 1: For each noun listed below, write **S** for singular or **P** for plural.

Noun	S or P	Noun	S or P	Noun	S or P
1. rabbits		5. families		9. ducks	
2. airplane		6. kite		10. men	
3. monkeys		7. trains		11. bird	
4. man		8. butterfly		12. doll	

Chapter 16, Lesson 3, Practice 2: Correct the capitalization mistakes and put the rule number above each correction. Use the rule numbers in Reference 11 on page 17 in the Reference Section of your book. Put a (.) or a (?) at the end of the sentence.

_____ **(capitalization rule numbers)**

i   am   leaving   on   monday   for   chicago,   illinois _____ **(4 capitals)**

Chapter 16, Lesson 3, Practice 3: On notebook paper, write a sentence using the words in the Word Bank. Put the words you select in the same order as the Sentence Labels listed below. Write the correct label above each word in your sentence.

WORD BANK

Nouns	Verbs	Adjectives	Adverbs	Prepositional Phrases
airplane helicopter jet	landed arrived flew	a, an, the, large, loud, new, swift, fast, big, blue, silver, army	promptly, carefully, safely, today, suddenly, around, rapidly	on time at the airport on the runway to the ship

Sentence Labels: A Adj SN V Adv Prep Phrase

Independent Exercise: Choose your own Sentence Labels.

Chapter 17, Lesson 1, Practice: For each noun listed below, write **C** for common or **P** for proper.

Noun	C or P	Noun	C or P	Noun	C or P
1. student		5. Ted		9. Easter	
2. Mr. Smith		6. England		10. cup	
3. city		7. boy		11. clock	
4. Kansas		8. Italy		12. map	

Chapter 17, Lesson 2, Practice: For each noun listed below, write **C** for common or **P** for proper.

Noun	C or P	Noun	C or P	Noun	C or P
1. Walker School		5. watch		9. Anna	
2. Mandy		6. cloud		10. mail	
3. milk		7. Mr. Jones		11. state	
4. tiger		8. August		12. Thanksgiving	

Chapter 17, Lesson 3, Practice 1: For each noun listed below, write **C** for common or **P** for proper.

Noun	C or P	Noun	C or P	Noun	C or P
1. cake		5. Monday		9. July	
2. Mr. Brown		6. James		10. Africa	
3. duck		7. key		11. Tuesday	
4. January		8. barn		12. desk	

Chapter 17, Lesson 3, Practice 2: For each noun listed below, write **S** for singular or **P** for plural.

Noun	S or P	Noun	S or P	Noun	S or P
1. friends		5. prunes		9. leg	
2. bug		6. games		10. arm	
3. stars		7. house		11. knee	
4. bushes		8. street		12. letters	

Chapter 17, Lesson 3, Practice 3: Correct the capitalization mistakes and put the rule number above each correction. Use the rule numbers in Reference 11 on page 17 in the Reference Section of your book. Put a (**.**) or a (**?**) at the end of the sentence.

_____ **(capitalization rule numbers)**

peter   will   arrive   in   oregon   next   tuesday _____ **(3 capitals)**

Chapter 18, Lesson 1, Practice 1: Write the name of the topic that best describes what each column of words is about. Choose from these topics:

Colors   City Things   Animals   Country Things   Shapes

(1)	(2)	(3)
_____	_____	_____
skyscraper	tractor	triangle
taxi	farm	square
subway	barn	circle

Level 1 Homeschool Student Book

Chapter 18, Lesson 1, Practice 2: In each column, cross out the one idea that does not support the underlined topic at the top.

(1) Kitchen Things	(2) Breakfast	(3) Birds
skillet	cereal	hawk
umpire	toast	eagle
oven	eggs	rat
spoon	automobile	robin

Chapter 18, Lesson 1, Practice 3: Read each topic. Then, cross out the one sentence that does not support the topic.

A. Topic: My Dog Buddy

1. My dog's name is Buddy.
2. Buddy likes to play fetch.
3. Buddy sleeps beside my bed at night.
4. My horse's name is Flash.

B. Topic: Summer Vacation

1. My family takes a vacation every summer.
2. This summer we are going to Hawaii.
3. We visited Grandmother on Thanksgiving.
4. Last summer, we went to Florida.

Chapter 18, Lesson 2, Practice 1: Correct the capitalization mistakes and put the rule number above each correction. Use the rule numbers in Reference 11 on page 17 in the Reference Section of your book. Put a (**.**) or a (**?**) at the end of the sentence.

_____ **(capitalization rule numbers)**

stephen   and   billy   will   travel   to   atlanta   in   february _____ **(4 capitals)**

Chapter 18, Lesson 2, Practice 2: Write the name of the topic that best describes what each column of words is about. Choose from these topics:

Colors	Transportation	Farm Animals	Kitchen Things	Green Things
(1)		(2)		(3)
_____		_____		_____
leaf		car		goat
grasshopper		truck		pig
grass		van		cow

Chapter 18, Lesson 2, Practice 3: In each column, cross out the one idea that does not support the underlined topic at the top.

(1) Flowers	(2) Clothing	(3) Yellow Things
rose	socks	banana
ocean	pants	school bus
daisy	skirt	lake
tulip	lamp	lemon

Chapter 18, Lesson 2, Practice 4: Read each topic. Then, cross out the one sentence that does not support the topic.

A. Topic: The Library

1. The library is full of wonderful books.
2. The library is open six days a week.
3. I like to borrow many books from the library.
4. I need to go grocery shopping today.

B. Topic: A Day at the Lake

1. Every summer, we spend a day at the lake.
2. We rent a boat early in the morning.
3. My brother got a new computer.
4. My dad and I ski behind the boat.

Chapter 18, Lesson 3, Practice 1: Write the name of the topic that best describes what each column of words is about. Choose from these topics:

Colors	Winter Things	Ocean Animals	Yellow Things	Summer Things
	(1)	(2)		(3)
	_____	_____		_____
	gloves	dolphin		sun
	coat	whale		butter
	snow	shark		corn

Chapter 18, Lesson 3, Practice 2: In each column, cross out the one idea that does not support the underlined topic at the top.

(1) People	(2) States	(3) Farm Words
police officer	Nevada	tractor
hippopotamus	Louisiana	plow
teacher	Vermont	plastic
mother	cheese	barn

Chapter 18, Lesson 3, Practice 3: Read each topic. Then, cross out the one sentence that does not support the topic.

A. Topic: Uncle David

1. Uncle David works on a farm.
2. Uncle David lives in Oklahoma.
3. Uncle David is my favorite uncle.
4. Aunt Rita works in a clothing factory.

B. Topic: Our House

1. We live in a small white house.
2. Our house is on Elm Street.
3. Joey lives in Dallas.
4. We have lived in our house for ten years.

Chapter 18, Lesson 3, Practice 4: Correct the capitalization mistakes and put the rule number above each correction. Use the rule numbers in Reference 11 on page 17 in the Reference Section of your book. Put a (**.**) or a (**?**) at the end of the sentence.

_____ (capitalization rule numbers)

jack   will   bring   punch   and   cookies   on   wednesday   night ____ **(2 capitals)**

Chapter 18, Lesson 3, Practice 5: On notebook paper, write a sentence using the words in the Word Bank. Put the words you select in the same order as the Sentence Labels listed below. Write the correct label above each word in your sentence.

WORD BANK

Nouns	Verbs	Adjectives	Adverbs	Prepositional Phrases
clown kite balloon friend	waved, shouted, soared, talked, floated, walked	a, an, the, silly, large, funny, best, old, new, giant, happy, green, silly	eagerly, high, excitedly, often, silently, loudly, today	to the children in the sky to the mall to the crowd

Sentence Labels: A Adj Adj SN V Adv Prep Phrase

Independent Exercise: Choose your own Sentence Labels and Words.

Chapter 18, Lesson 4, Practice 1: Write the name of the topic that best describes what each column of words is about. Choose from these topics:

Numbers	Table Things	Animals	Weather Words	Drinks
(1)		(2)		(3)
_____		_____		_____
cloudy		eight		punch
rainy		two		soda
windy		three		juice

Chapter 18, Lesson 4, Practice 2: In each column, cross out the one idea that does not support the underlined topic at the top.

(1) Brown Things	(2) Beans	(3) Vegetables
dirt	refried	carrots
sky	green	squash
chocolate	pinto	gravy
otter	mail	broccoli

Chapter 18, Lesson 4, Practice 3: Read each topic. Then, cross out the one sentence that does not support the topic.

A. Topic: Happiness

1. Happiness is being with my mom.
2. Happiness is a warm hug.
3. Happiness is a beautiful rainbow.
4. Scary movies frighten me.

B. Topic: My New Shoes

1. My new shoes are white.
2. My new shoes feel comfortable on my feet.
3. My old shoes were black.
4. My new shoes have purple laces.

Chapter 18, Lesson 4, Practice 4: Correct the capitalization mistakes and put the rule number above each correction. Use the rule numbers in Reference 11 on page 17 in the Reference Section of your book. Put a (.) or a (?) at the end of the sentence.

_____ **(capitalization rule numbers)**

may   i   have   another   piece   of   janet's   pie _____ **(3 capitals)**

Chapter 19, Lesson 1, Practice: Use Writing Outline 1 for Writing Assignment #1. Use this two-point outline form to guide you as you write a two-point expository paragraph.

Writing Outline 1

Write a topic: _____

Write 2 points to list about the topic.

1. _____   2. _____

Sentence #1 Topic sentence (*Use words in the topic and tell how many points will be used.*)

_____

_____

Sentence #2 2-point sentence (*List your 2 points in the order that you will present them.*)

_____

_____

Sentence #3 State your first point in a complete sentence.

_____

_____

Sentence #4 Write a supporting sentence for the first point.

_____

_____

Sentence #5 State your second point in a complete sentence.

_____

_____

Sentence #6 Write a supporting sentence for the second point.

_____

_____

Sentence #7 Concluding sentence (*Restate the topic sentence and add an extra thought.*)

_____

_____

Chapter 19, Lesson 4, Practice: Use Writing Outline 2 for Writing Assignment #2. Use this two-point outline form to guide you as you write a two-point expository paragraph.

Writing Outline 2

Write a topic: _____

Write 2 points to list about the topic.

1. _____   2. _____

Sentence #1 Topic sentence (*Use words in the topic and tell how many points will be used.*)

_____

_____

Sentence #2 2-point sentence (*List your 2 points in the order that you will present them.*)

_____

_____

Sentence #3 State your first point in a complete sentence.

_____

_____

Sentence #4 Write a supporting sentence for the first point.

_____

_____

Sentence #5 State your second point in a complete sentence.

_____

_____

Sentence #6 Write a supporting sentence for the second point.

_____

_____

Sentence #7 Concluding sentence (*Restate the topic sentence and add an extra thought.*)

_____

_____

Chapter 21, Lesson 1, Practice: Write **S** for a complete sentence and **F** for a sentence fragment on the line beside each group of words below.

_____ 1. The cookies baked in the oven.

_____ 2. Bells rang.

_____ 3. A brown camel.

_____ 4. That new book.

_____ 5. Watches baseball.

_____ 6. Across the street.

_____ 7. Every soldier waited for orders.

_____ 8. Tray rode his new bicycle.

_____ 9. Circled the tall tower.

_____ 10. A painted pony.

_____ 11. The driver stopped quickly.

_____ 12. At the park.

_____ 13. The children played in the yard.

_____ 14. In the end.

_____ 15. Flowers in the garden.

Chapter 21, Lesson 2, Practice 1: Match each subject part with the correct predicate part by writing the correct sentence number in the blank.

1. A horse _____ was in a new movie.

2. The wildflowers _____ was printed yesterday.

3. The newspaper _____ galloped through the pasture.

4. That actor _____ appeared above the trees.

5. The beautiful rainbow _____ bloomed in the field.

Chapter 21, Lesson 2, Practice 2: Write **S** for a complete sentence and **F** for a sentence fragment on the line beside each group of words below.

_____ 1. A curious raccoon.

_____ 2. Travis walked to the store.

_____ 3. Lives in the alley.

_____ 4. This broken toy.

_____ 5. The soup cooked.

_____ 6. People in the stands.

_____ 7. The couple sat on the couch.

_____ 8. Jamie parked her car in the garage.

_____ 9. Five new kittens.

_____ 10. I did well on the test.

Chapter 21, Lesson 3, Practice 1: Match each subject part with the correct predicate part by writing the correct sentence number in the blank.

1. The glass vase   _____ fit nicely.

2. The dentist   _____ chased the robber.

3. Five police officers   _____ shattered on the floor.

4. My Easter dress   _____ squeezed under the fence.

5. A bunny   _____ cleaned my teeth.

Chapter 21, Lesson 3, Practice 2: Write **S** for a complete sentence and **F** for a sentence fragment on the line beside each group of words below.

_____	1. An empty box.
_____	2. We swam across the pool.
_____	3. Flies a plane.
_____	4. I talked with Susan.
_____	5. Near the end of the road.
_____	6. Trapped in the cave.
_____	7. Ball rolled.
_____	8. The rain fell hard.
_____	9. The two churches.
_____	10. The children ran fast.

Chapter 22, Lesson 1, Practice 1: Write the correct contraction in each blank.

1. are not	_____	5. is not	_____
2. is not	_____	6. are not	_____
3. was not	_____	7. were not	_____
4. were not	_____	8. was not	_____

Chapter 22, Lesson 1, Practice 2: Write the correct words beside each contraction.

1. aren't	_____	5. isn't	_____
2. isn't	_____	6. aren't	_____
3. wasn't	_____	7. weren't	_____
4. weren't	_____	8. wasn't	_____

Chapter 22, Lesson 1, Practice 3: Underline the correct contraction at the right for the words that are underlined in each sentence. Use Reference 24 on page 21 to help you.

1. My crayons <u>are not</u> missing.	isn't	aren't
2. His pencil <u>is not</u> sharp.	isn't	aren't
3. The books <u>are not</u> expensive.	isn't	aren't
4. The officer <u>was not</u> here.	wasn't	weren't
5. My brother <u>was not</u> ill.	wasn't	weren't
6. My notes <u>were not</u> in order.	wasn't	weren't

Chapter 22, Lesson 1, Practice 4: Write the correct contraction in the blank for the words that are underlined in each sentence. Use Reference 24 on page 21 to help you.

1. The bread <u>was not</u> fresh. _____

2. My clothes <u>are not</u> packed. _____

3. The students <u>were not</u> on time. _____

4. The baby <u>is not</u> happy. _____

Chapter 22, Lesson 2, Practice 1: Write the correct contraction in each blank. Use Reference 25 on page 22 to help you.

1. I am _____   4. does not _____

2. cannot _____   5. did not _____

3. do not _____

Chapter 22, Lesson 2, Practice 2: Write the correct words beside each contraction. Use Reference 25 on page 22 to help you.

1. didn't _____
2. can't _____
3. doesn't _____

4. I'm _____
5. don't _____

Chapter 22, Lesson 2, Practice 3: Write the correct contraction in the blank for the words that are underlined in each sentence. Use Reference 25 on page 22 to help you.

1. My mother knows that I am responsible. _____
2. Those boys cannot play. _____
3. The rain did not stop for days. _____
4. His room does not need to be cleaned. _____
5. The stores do not open today. _____

Chapter 22, Lesson 3, Practice 1: Write the correct contraction in each blank. Use the contraction references to help you. Use Reference 25 on page 22 to help you.

1. do not _____
2. cannot _____
3. were not _____
4. I am _____

5. are not _____
6. is not _____
7. did not _____
8. does not _____

Chapter 22, Lesson 3, Practice 2: Write the correct words beside each contraction. Use the contraction references to help you.

1. I'm _____
2. isn't _____
3. doesn't _____
4. wasn't _____

5. weren't _____
6. can't _____
7. didn't _____
8. aren't _____

Chapter 22, Lesson 3, Practice 3: Write the correct contraction in the blank for the words that are underlined in each sentence. Use the contraction references to help you.

1. The machines <u>are not</u> broken. _____

2. I <u>cannot</u> play the tuba. _____

3. The students <u>did not</u> read the directions. _____

4. Harry <u>does not</u> play basketball. _____

5. The numbers <u>do not</u> make sense. _____

6. Jill knows that <u>I am</u> busy. _____

7. Kathy <u>is not</u> coming to my party. _____

8. Patrick <u>was not</u> paying attention. _____

9. The fans <u>were not</u> allowed on the field. _____

Chapter 23, Lesson 1, Practice 1: Identify the tense of each underlined verb by writing a number **1** for past tense, a number **2** for present tense, or a number **3** for future tense.

Verb Tense	Regular Verbs	Verb Tense	Irregular Verbs
	1. Kelly <u>will play</u> with her dolls.		7. The sisters <u>take</u> piano lessons.
	2. Kelly <u>played</u> with her dolls.		8. The sisters <u>will take</u> piano lessons.
	3. Kelly <u>plays</u> with her dolls.		9. The sisters <u>took</u> piano lessons.
	4. The hockey players <u>skate</u>.		10. Mary <u>buys</u> a blue dress.
	5. The hockey players <u>will skate</u>.		11. Mary <u>will buy</u> a blue dress.
	6. The hockey players <u>skated</u>.		12. Mary <u>bought</u> a blue dress.

Chapter 23, Lesson 1, Practice 2: Chant the following verbs to hear the different tenses.

Regular Verbs			Irregular Verbs		
listened	listen	will listen	bought	buy	will buy
talked	talk	will talk	took	take	will take
skated	skate	will skate	drove	drive	will drive
played	play	will play	sold	sell	will sell

Chapter 23, Lesson 2, Practice: Identify the tense of each underlined verb by writing a number **1** for past tense, a number **2** for present tense, or a number **3** for future tense.

Verb Tense	Regular Verbs	Verb Tense	Irregular Verbs
	1. Tim will jump into the pool.		6. Jim drives to church.
	2. Tim jumped into the pool.		7. Jim will drive to church.
	3. Tim jumps into the pool.		8. Jim drove to church.
	4. Mom yells loudly for our team.		9. She will sing for a large audience.
	5. Mom will yell loudly for our team.		10. She sings for a large audience.

Chapter 23, Lesson 3, Practice: Identify the tense of each underlined verb by writing a number **1** for past tense, a number **2** for present tense, or a number **3** for future tense.

Verb Tense	Regular Verbs	Verb Tense	Irregular Verbs
	1. The truck will back into the ditch.		6. Grandma speaks softly.
	2. The truck backed into the ditch.		7. Grandma will speak softly.
	3. The truck backs into the ditch.		8. Grandma spoke softly.
	4. The planes circle the runway.		9. The workers dig a deep hole.
	5. The planes will circle the runway.		10. The workers dug a deep hole.

Chapter 24, Lesson 1, Practice: Write the parts of a friendly letter in the correct places in the friendly letter below.

1. Heading
19 Dogwood Lane
Benton, KS 24550
July 23, 20_____

2. Greeting
Dear Samuel,

3. Closing
Your friend,

4. Signature
Ruth

5. Body
We just got back from our trip to Alaska. It was so much fun. I have so much to tell you!

Friendly Letter

Heading
_____
_____
_____

Greeting
_____

Body

Closing
_____

Signature

Chapter 24, Lesson 2, Practice 1: Identify the tense of each underlined verb by writing a number **1** for past tense, a number **2** for present tense, or a number **3** for future tense.

Verb Tense	Regular Verbs	Verb Tense	Irregular Verbs
	1. The band <u>will march</u> in the parade.		4. The ship <u>sinks</u> quickly.
	2. The band <u>marched</u> in the parade.		5. The ship <u>will sink</u> quickly.
	3. The band <u>marches</u> in the parade.		6. The ship <u>sank</u> quickly.

Chapter 24, Lesson 2, Practice 2: On notebook paper, write a friendly letter to a friend or relative. Use References 27 and 28 as a guide to make sure your letter is in the correct friendly-letter format. Have your parents help you address an envelope. Mail your letter and wait for a response.

Chapter 24, Lesson 3, Practice 1: Identify the tense of each underlined verb by writing a number **1** for past tense, a number **2** for present tense, or a number **3** for future tense.

Verb Tense	Regular Verbs	Verb Tense	Irregular Verbs
	1. The cookies <u>will bake</u> in the oven.		4. The choir <u>will sing</u> in the early service.
	2. The cookies <u>bake</u> in the oven.		5. The choir <u>sang</u> in the early service.
	3. The cookies <u>baked</u> in the oven.		6. The choir <u>sings</u> in the early service.

Chapter 24, Lesson 3, Practice 2: On notebook paper, write a friendly letter to a friend or relative. Use References 27 and 28 as a guide to make sure your letter is in the correct friendly-letter format. Have your parents help you address an envelope. Mail your letter and wait for a response.

Chapter 25, Lesson 1, Practice: First, think of a person who has done something nice for you or has given you a gift (even the gift of time). On notebook paper, write a thank-you note to that person. Use the information in Reference 29 or 30 as a guide. Have your parents help you address an envelope. Mail your thank-you note.

Chapter 25, Lesson 2, Practice 1: Identify the tense of each underlined verb by writing a number **1** for past tense, a number **2** for present tense, or a number **3** for future tense.

Verb Tense	Regular Verbs	Verb Tense	Irregular Verbs
	1. The road <u>will curve</u> around the lake.		4. The author <u>wrote</u> a new play.
	2. The road <u>curved</u> around the lake.		5. The author <u>writes</u> a new play.
	3. The road <u>curves</u> around the lake.		6. The author <u>will write</u> a new play.

Chapter 25, Lesson 2, Practice 2: First, think of a person who has done something nice for you or has given you a gift (even the gift of time). On notebook paper, write a thank-you note to that person. Use the information in Reference 29 or 30 as a guide. Have your parents help you address an envelope. Mail your thank-you note.

Chapter 25, Lesson 3, Practice 1: Identify the tense of each underlined verb by writing a number **1** for past tense, a number **2** for present tense, or a number **3** for future tense.

Verb Tense	Regular Verbs	Verb Tense	Irregular Verbs
	1. Billy will wash the dishes.		4. The players shake hands.
	2. Billy washed the dishes.		5. The players will shake hands.
	3. Billy washes the dishes.		6. The players shook hands.

Chapter 25, Lesson 3, Practice 2: Think of a person who has done something nice for you or has given you a gift (even the gift of time). On notebook paper, write a thank-you note to that person. Use the information in Reference 29 or 30 as a guide. Have your parents help you address an envelope. Mail your thank-you note.

Chapter 26, Lesson 1, Practice: Put each group of words in alphabetical order. Write numbers in the blanks to show the order in each column.

Winter Words	Family Words	"S" Words	Fruit Words
_____ 1. snow	_____ 4. sister	_____ 7. ship	_____ 10. banana
_____ 2. ice	_____ 5. father	_____ 8. sun	_____ 11. apple
_____ 3. coat	_____ 6. aunt	_____ 9. seven	_____ 12. orange

Chapter 26, Lesson 2, Practice 1: Write the letters in each group below in alphabetical order.

1. g o c w _____

2. x f n k a t _____

Chapter 26, Lesson 2, Practice 2: Put each group of words in alphabetical order. Write numbers in the blanks to show the order in each column.

Space Words	City Words	"R" Words
_____ 1. stars	_____ 3. park	_____ 5. rabbit
_____ 2. moon	_____ 4. skyscraper	_____ 6. road

Chapter 26, Lesson 2, Practice 3: Put each group of words in alphabetical order. Write numbers in the blanks to show the order in each column.

Summer Words	"T" Words	Vegetable Words
_____ 1. sunscreen	_____ 4. tank	_____ 7. corn
_____ 2. swimsuit	_____ 5. toy	_____ 8. potato
_____ 3. vacation	_____ 6. two	_____ 9. carrot

Chapter 26, Lesson 3, Practice 1: Write the letters in each group below in alphabetical order.

1. b   w   j   m   _____

2. z   p   a   u   o   e   _____

Chapter 26, Lesson 3, Practice 2: Put each group of words in alphabetical order. Write numbers in the blanks to show the order in each column.

State Words	Ocean Words	"O" Words
_____ 1. Alaska	_____ 3. waves	_____ 5. otter
_____ 2. Arizona	_____ 4. whale	_____ 6. old

Chapter 26, Lesson 3, Practice 3: Put each group of words in alphabetical order. Write numbers in the blanks to show the order in each column.

Breakfast Words	"D" Words	Movie Words
_____ 1. toast	_____ 4. duck	_____ 7. popcorn
_____ 2. eggs	_____ 5. donkey	_____ 8. soda
_____ 3. milk	_____ 6. dog	_____ 9. candy

Chapter 26, Lesson 4, Practice 1: Write the letters in each group below in alphabetical order.

1. l h r c   _____

2. f i k o w r   _____

Chapter 26, Lesson 4, Practice 2: Put each group of words in alphabetical order. Write numbers in the blanks to show the order in each column.

Transportation Words	Tool Words	"J" Words
_____ 1. bus	_____ 3. drill	_____ 5. jet
_____ 2. boat	_____ 4. hammer	_____ 6. jelly

Chapter 26, Lesson 4, Practice 3: Put each group of words in alphabetical order. Write numbers in the blanks to show the order in each column.

Hospital Words	"D" Words	Clothing Words
_____ 1. nurse	_____ 4. deer	_____ 7. shirt
_____ 2. patient	_____ 5. duck	_____ 8. skirt
_____ 3. doctor	_____ 6. dog	_____ 9. sweater

Chapter 27, Lesson 3, Practice 1: Underline the correct answer in each sentence.

1. Nonfiction books contain information and stories that are (**true, not true**).
2. Fiction books contain information and stories that are (**true, not true**).
3. The most common reference books are the dictionary and the encyclopedia.
   (**true, not true**)

Chapter 27, Lesson 3, Practice 2: Put each group of words in alphabetical order. Write numbers in the blanks to show the order in each column.

Adjective Words	"G" Words	Cleaning Words
_____ 1. squirmy	_____ 4. grasshopper	_____ 7. rags
_____ 2. strong	_____ 5. goats	_____ 8. broom
_____ 3. silly	_____ 6. giant	_____ 9. mop

Chapter 27, Lesson 4, Practice 1: Underline the correct answer in each sentence.

1. Nonfiction books contain information and stories that are (**true, not true**).
2. Fiction books contain information and stories that are (**true, not true**).
3. The most common reference books are the dictionary and the encyclopedia.
   (**true, not true**)

Chapter 27, Lesson 4, Practice 2: Put each group of words in alphabetical order. Write numbers in the blanks to show the order in each column.

Preposition Words	Verb Words	Pet Words
_____ 1. in	_____ 4. erupted	_____ 7. pony
_____ 2. to	_____ 5. camped	_____ 8. cat
_____ 3. on	_____ 6. yawned	_____ 9. dog

TEST

SECTION

Chapter 7 Test

Exercise 1: Classify each sentence. Use **SN** for subject noun, **V** for verb, and **Adv** for adverb.

1. Cats jumped quickly.
   SN V Adv

2. Puppies played quietly yesterday.
   SN V Adv Adv

Exercise 2: Underline the **syn** if the words are synonyms. Underline the **ant** if the words are antonyms.

1. in, out	syn ant	2. quit, stop	syn ant	3. right, wrong	syn ant

---

Exercise 3: In your journal, write a paragraph summarizing what you have learned this week.

I am going out side.

Andrew did a great job on his test!

Chapter 8 Test

A+

Exercise 1: Classify each sentence. Use **SN** for subject noun, **V** for verb, **Adv** for adverb, and **Adj** for adjective.

1. Adv Adj SN V Adv Adv
   Three squirmy puppies barked loudly today.

2. Adj Adj SN V Adv Adv
   Two brown ducks sat quietly yesterday.

Exercise 2: Underline the **syn** if the words are synonyms. Underline the **ant** if the words are antonyms.

1. stone, rock	syn ant	2. warm, cold	syn ant	3. over, under	syn ant

Exercise 3: In your journal, write a paragraph summarizing what you have learned this week.

Austin waz plade
a2 Jeasus atLIT.

Austin played as Jesus
at LIT.

Chapter 9 Test

Exercise 1: Classify each sentence. Use **SN** for subject noun, **V** for verb, **Adv** for adverb, **Adj** for adjective, and **A** for article adjective.

1.
    A   Adv   Adj   SN   V   Abv   Abv
    The   three   yellow   cats   walked   quietly today.

2.
    A   Adj   SN   V   Abv   Adv
    A   brown   horse   raced   quickly   away.

Exercise 2: Underline the **syn** if the words are synonyms. Underline the **ant** if the words are antonyms.

1. start, begin	syn ant	2. up, down	syn ant	3. push, pull	syn ant

---

Exercise 3: Name the four parts of speech that you have studied. (*You may use abbreviations.*)

1. SN   2. V   3. Adj   4. Abv

Exercise 4: In your journal, write a paragraph summarizing what you have learned this week.

I learned to classify article adjectives.

Chapter 10 Test

Exercise 1: Classify each sentence. Use **SN** for subject noun, **V** for verb, **Adv** for adverb, **Adj** for adjective, and **A** for article adjective. For Sentence 1, underline the complete subject <u>one</u> time and the complete predicate <u>two</u> times.

1.   A   Adj   Adj   SN   V   Adv   Adv
The five big ships sailed home yesterday.

2.   A   Adj   SN   V   Adv   Adv
An excited dog barked loudly today.

Exercise 2: Underline the **syn** if the words are synonyms. Underline the **ant** if the words are antonyms.

1. front, back	syn <u>ant</u>	2. rough, smooth	syn <u>ant</u>	3. giant, huge	<u>syn</u> ant

Exercise 3: Name the four parts of speech that you have studied. (*You may use abbreviations.*)

1. Noun   2. verb   3. Adjective 4. Adverb

Exercise 4: In your journal, write a paragraph summarizing what you have learned this week.

Chapter 11 Test

Exercise 1: Classify each sentence. Use **SN** for subject noun, **V** for verb, **Adv** for adverb, **Adj** for adjective, and **A** for article adjective. For Sentence 2, underline the complete subject <u>one</u> time and the complete predicate <u>two</u> times

1.   The   three   silly   clowns   ran   around   happily.

2.   A   beautiful   black   car   stopped   suddenly.

Exercise 2: Underline the **syn** if the words are synonyms. Underline the **ant** if the words are antonyms.

1. inside, outside	**syn ant**	2. form, shape	**syn ant**	3. end, finish	**syn ant**

Exercise 3: Name the four parts of speech that you have studied. (*You may use abbreviations.*)

1. _____ 2. _____ 3. _____ 4. _____

Exercise 4: On notebook paper, write each sentence correctly. Capitalize the first word of each sentence and put a (**.**) or a (**?**) at the end.

1.   the   yellow   cab   stopped   suddenly

2.   did   the   home   team   win   yesterday

Exercise 5: On notebook paper, write a sentence using the words in the Word Bank. Put the words you select in the same order as the Sentence Labels listed below. Write the correct label above each word in your sentence.

WORD BANK			
Nouns	**Verbs**	**Adjectives**	**Adverbs**
bird ant snake	scurried, climbed, crawled, flew, ate, slithered, hopped	a, an, the, two, busy, tiny, hungry, huge, green, pretty, yellow, black, funny, little, excited	hastily, slowly, quickly, suddenly, fast, today, silently, around, early, away
Sentence Labels: A Adj SN V Adv		(Bonus) A Adj Adj SN V Adv Adv	

Exercise 6: In your journal, write a paragraph summarizing what you have learned this week.

Chapter 12 Test

Exercise 1: Classify each sentence. Use **SN** for subject noun, **V** for verb, **Adv** for adverb, **Adj** for adjective, and **A** for article adjective. For Sentence 2, underline the complete subject <u>one</u> time and the complete predicate <u>two</u> times

1.   The   red   flowers   grew   rapidly.

2.   Six   large   jets   flew   fast   today.

Exercise 2: Underline the <u>syn</u> if the words are synonyms. Underline the <u>ant</u> if the words are antonyms.

1. open, close	syn ant	2. tiny, small	syn ant	3. high, low	syn ant

Exercise 3: Name the four parts of speech that you have studied. (*You may use abbreviations.*)

1. _____ 2. _____ 3. _____ 4. _____

Exercise 4: Write *a* or *an* in the blanks.

1. The cat chased _____ ant.   3. Pat carved _____ pumpkin.   5. ____ arm   7. ____ insect

2. We made _____ cake.   4. The house has _____ door.   6. ____ mat   8. ____ elevator

Exercise 5: On notebook paper, write a sentence using the words in the Word Bank. Put the words you select in the same order as the Sentence Labels listed below. Write the correct label above each word in your sentence.

WORD BANK			
Nouns	**Verbs**	**Adjectives**	**Adverbs**
men women students	walked, laughed, ran, talked, fished, looked, shouted, stopped, worked, yawned, drove	a, an, the, several, young, friendly, big, happy, cheerful, busy, weary, tired, frightened, eager, excited	easily, happily, quietly, slowly, suddenly, today, rapidly, away, carefully, early, loudly
Sentence Labels: A Adj SN V Adv (Bonus) A Adj Adj SN V Adv Adv			

Exercise 6: In your journal, write a paragraph summarizing what you have learned this week.

Chapter 13 Test

Exercise 1: Classify each sentence. Use **SN** for subject noun, **V** for verb, **Adv** for adverb, **Adj** for adjective, **A** for article adjective, **P** for preposition, and **OP** for object of the preposition. For Sentence 1, underline the complete subject <u>one</u> time and the complete predicate <u>two</u> times.

1.   The   busy   little   bee   landed   softly   on   the   flower.

2.   The   poor   girl   fell   in   the   mud.

Exercise 2: Underline the **<u>syn</u>** if the words are synonyms. Underline the **<u>ant</u>** if the words are antonyms.

1. part, piece	syn ant	2. far, near	syn ant	3. rush, hurry	syn ant

---

Exercise 3: Name the five parts of speech that you have studied. (*You may use abbreviations.*)

1. _____ 2. _____ 3. _____ 4. _____ 5. _____

Exercise 4: Write *a* or *an* in the blanks.

1. He was stranded on _____ island.   3. Pat planted _____ garden.   5. _____ odor   7. _____ eel

2. I saw _____ deer in the woods.   4. The birds built _____ nest.   6. _____ jar   8. _____ album

Exercise 5: In your journal, write a paragraph summarizing what you have learned this week.

Chapter 14 Test

Exercise 1: Classify each sentence. Use **SN** for subject noun, **V** for verb, **Adv** for adverb, **Adj** for adjective, **A** for article adjective, **P** for preposition, and **OP** for object of the preposition. For Sentence 1, underline the complete subject <u>one</u> time and the complete predicate <u>two</u> times.

1. The   beautiful   music   played   softly   in   the   store.

2. A   frightened   brown   duck   flew   across   the   road   today.

Exercise 2: Underline the <u>syn</u> if the words are synonyms. Underline the <u>ant</u> if the words are antonyms.

1. old, new	**syn ant**	2. lean, thin	**syn ant**	3. above, below	**syn ant**

Exercise 3: Name the five parts of speech that you have studied. (*You may use abbreviations.*)

1. _____   2. _____   3. _____   4. _____   5. _____

Exercise 4: Write *a* or *an* in the blanks.

1. Jan boiled _____ egg.   3. The actor wore _____ mask.   5. _____ officer   7. _____ eye

2. He works in _____ factory.   4. Lisa ate _____ apple.   6. _____ fire   8. _____ napkin

---

Exercise 5: On notebook paper, write a sentence using the words in the Word Bank. Put the words you select in the same order as the Sentence Labels listed below. Write the correct label above each word in your sentence.

WORD BANK				
Nouns	**Verbs**	**Adjectives**	**Adverbs**	**Prepositional Phrases**
teacher coaches friend	waved smiled talked	a, an, the, friendly, busy, new, eager, several, enthusiastic	warmly, patiently, happily, today	at the children to the parents to the players
Sentence Labels: A Adj Adj SN V Adv Prep Phrase				

Exercise 6: In your journal, write a paragraph summarizing what you have learned this week.

Chapter 15 Test

Exercise 1: Classify each sentence. Use **SN** for subject noun, **V** for verb, **Adv** for adverb, **Adj** for adjective, **A** for article adjective, **P** for preposition, and **OP** for object of the preposition. For Sentence 1, underline the complete subject <u>one</u> time and the complete predicate <u>two</u> times.

1. The   eight   shivering   puppies   whimpered   loudly.

2. The   big   ocean   waves   crashed   loudly   across   the   rocks.

Exercise 2: Underline the <u>**syn**</u> if the words are synonyms. Underline the <u>**ant**</u> if the words are antonyms.

1. left, right	**syn ant**	2. poor, rich	**syn ant**	3. puzzle, riddle	**syn ant**

Exercise 3: Name the five parts of speech that you have studied. (*You may use abbreviations.*)

1. _____   2. _____   3. _____   4. _____   5. _____

Exercise 4: Correct the capitalization mistakes and put the rule number above each correction. Use the rule numbers in Reference 11 on page 17 in the Reference Section of your book. Put a (**.**) or a (**?**) at the end of the sentence.

_____(capitalization rule numbers)

i   will   ride   to   school   with   katie   on   tuesday ____ (3 capitals)

Exercise 5: On notebook paper, write a sentence using the words in the Word Bank. Put the words you select in the same order as the Sentence Labels listed below. Write the correct label above each word in your sentence.

WORD BANK				
Nouns	**Verbs**	**Adjectives**	**Adverbs**	**Prepositional Phrases**
fox squirrel raccoon	peeked stared glanced	a, an, the, baby, cute, tiny, tired, red, large, frisky, curious, hungry, playful	suddenly excitedly cautiously curiously	in the box at the boy at the house across the yard
Sentence Labels: A Adj Adj SN V Adv Prep Phrase				

Exercise 6: In your journal, write a paragraph summarizing what you have learned this week.

Chapter 16 Test

Exercise 1: Classify each sentence. Use **SN** for subject noun, **V** for verb, **Adv** for adverb, **Adj** for adjective, **A** for article adjective, **P** for preposition, and **OP** for object of the preposition. For Sentence 1, underline the complete subject one time and the complete predicate two times.

1. Nine   yellow   kites   flew   silently   across   the   lake.

2. The   huge   rocks   rolled   suddenly   down   the   mountain.

Exercise 2: Underline the **syn** if the words are synonyms. Underline the **ant** if the words are antonyms.

| 1. on, off | syn ant | 2. tall, short | syn ant | 3. kind, good | syn ant |

Exercise 3: Name the five parts of speech that you have studied. (*You may use abbreviations.*)

1. _____   2. _____   3. _____   4. _____   5. _____

Exercise 4: Correct the capitalization mistakes and put the rule number above each correction. Use the rule numbers in Reference 11 on page 17 in the Reference Section of your book. Put a (**.**) or a (**?**) at the end of the sentence.

_____ (capitalization rule numbers)

does   walter   live   in   miami,   florida _____ (4 capitals)

Exercise 5: For each noun listed below, write **S** for singular or **P** for plural.

Noun	S or P	Noun	S or P	Noun	S or P
1. bats		5. boys		9. parrot	
2. woman		6. lady		10. children	
3. nests		7. women		11. piano	
4. apple		8. child		12. telephones	

Exercise 6: In your journal, write a paragraph summarizing what you have learned this week.

Chapter 17 Test

Exercise 1: Classify each sentence. Use **SN** for subject noun, **V** for verb, **Adv** for adverb, **Adj** for adjective, **A** for article adjective, **P** for preposition, and **OP** for object of the preposition. For Sentence 2, underline the complete subject <u>one</u> time and the complete predicate <u>two</u> times.

1.   The   big   volcano   erupted   suddenly   yesterday.

2.   Several   dogs   barked   loudly   at   the   car.

Exercise 2: Underline the **<u>syn</u>** if the words are synonyms. Underline the **<u>ant</u>** if the words are antonyms.

1. top, bottom	syn ant	2. evil, bad	syn ant	3. hard, firm	syn ant

---

Exercise 3: Name the five parts of speech that you have studied. (*You may use abbreviations.*)

1. _____   2. _____   3. _____   4. _____   5. _____

Exercise 4: Correct the capitalization mistakes and put the rule number above each correction. Use the rule numbers in Reference 11 on page 17 in the Reference Section of your book. Put a (.) or a (?) at the end of the sentence.

_____(capitalization rule numbers)

i   would   like   to   visit   alex   in   march ____   (3 capitals)

Exercise 5: Write **S** for singular or **P** for plural.

Noun	S or P
1. jar	
2. notebooks	
3. computer	
4. mice	

Exercise 6: Write **C** for Common or **P** for proper.

Noun	C or P
1. Mississippi	
2. James	
3. nephew	
4. window	

Exercise 7: In your journal, write a paragraph summarizing what you have learned this week.

Chapter 18 Test

Exercise 1: Classify each sentence. Use **SN** for subject noun, **V** for verb, **Adv** for adverb, **Adj** for adjective, **A** for article adjective, **P** for preposition, and **OP** for object of the preposition. For Sentence 1, underline the complete subject <u>one</u> time and the complete predicate <u>two</u> times.

1. The excited children played in the snow today.

2. Pink flowers grew by the gate.

Exercise 2: Underline the **<u>syn</u>** if the words are synonyms. Underline the **<u>ant</u>** if the words are antonyms.

1. sick, ill	**syn ant**	2. before, after	**syn ant**	3. lost, found	**syn ant**

Exercise 3: Name the five parts of speech that you have studied. (*You may use abbreviations.*)

1. _____ 2. _____ 3. _____ 4. _____ 5. _____

Exercise 4: Write the name of the topic that best describes what each column of words is about. Choose from these topics: **Colors   Family   Animals   Bathroom Things   Food**

(1)	(2)	(3)
_____	_____	_____
bread	uncle	shower
meat	cousin	shampoo
pasta	sister	towel

Exercise 5: In each column, cross out the one idea that does not support the underlined topic at the top.

(1)	(2)	(3)
Months	**Desserts**	**Days**
July	pie	Saturday
jail	cake	Wednesday
January	cookie	France
June	playground	Thursday

Exercise 6: Read each topic. Then, cross out the one sentence that does not support the topic.

A. Topic: My Favorite Color

1. My favorite color is yellow.
2. Yellow reminds me of sunshine.
3. I painted my room yellow.
4. Red and blue make purple.

B. Topic: In the City

1. I take a taxi to work every day in the city.
2. My apartment in the city is on the fifth floor.
3. I grew up in the country.
4. I have lived in the city for three years.

Exercise 7: In your journal, write a paragraph summarizing what you have learned this week.

Chapter 19 Test

Exercise 1: Classify each sentence. Use **SN** for subject noun, **V** for verb, **Adv** for adverb, **Adj** for adjective, **A** for article adjective, **P** for preposition, and **OP** for object of the preposition. For Sentence 1, underline the complete subject <u>one</u> time and the complete predicate <u>two</u> times.

1.   The   kind   nurse   talked   quietly   to   the   patient.

2.   The   three   busy   brothers   worked   hard.

Exercise 2: Underline the <u>syn</u> if the words are synonyms. Underline the <u>ant</u> if the words are antonyms.

1. front, back	syn ant	2. simple, easy	syn ant	3. early, late	syn ant

Exercise 3: Name the five parts of speech that you have studied. (*You may use abbreviations.*)

1. _____   2. _____   3. _____   4. _____   5. _____

Exercise 4: Correct the capitalization mistakes and put the rule number above each correction. Use the rule numbers in Reference 11 on page 17 in the Reference Section of your book. Put a (**.**) or a (**?**) at the end of the sentence.

_____(capitalization rule numbers)

does   bob   work   at   a   factory   in   jefferson   city,   missouri ____ (5 capitals)

Exercise 5: Write the name of the topic that best describes what each column of words is about. Choose from these topics: **Colors**   **Clothing**   **Animals**   **Kitchen Things**   **Plants**

(1)	(2)	(3)
_____	_____	_____
deer	sweater	tree
swan	shorts	grass
bear	shirts	flowers

Exercise 6: In each column, cross out the one idea that does not support the underlined topic at the top.

(1) School Supplies	(2) Winter Weather	(3) People
paper	snow	customer
turkey	sleet	teenager
pencil	ice	pickle
ruler	chicken	sister

Exercise 7: In your journal, write a paragraph summarizing what you have learned this week.

Chapter 20 Test

Exercise 1: Classify each sentence. Use **SN** for subject noun, **V** for verb, **Adv** for adverb, **Adj** for adjective, **A** for article adjective, **P** for preposition, and **OP** for object of the preposition. For Sentence 2, underline the complete subject <u>one</u> time and the complete predicate <u>two</u> times.

1.   The   three   friends   raced   excitedly   to   the   boat.

2.   The   cute   little   fireflies   glowed   brightly   in   the   dark.

Exercise 2: Underline the <u>syn</u> if the words are synonyms. Underline the <u>ant</u> if the words are antonyms.

1. slow, quick   **syn   ant**   2. first, last   **syn   ant**   3. raise, lift   **syn   ant**

Exercise 3: Name the five parts of speech that you have studied. (*You may use abbreviations.*)

1. _____   2. _____   3. _____   4. _____   5. _____

Exercise 4: Correct the capitalization mistakes and put the rule number above each correction. Use the rule numbers in Reference 11 on page 17 in the Reference Section of your book. Put a (**.**) or a (**?**) at the end of the sentence.

_____**(capitalization rule numbers)**

our   company   meets   in   tulsa   on   the   second   friday   in   july ____ **(4 capitals)**

Exercise 5: Write the name of the topic that best describes what each column of words is about. Choose from these topics: **Colors   People   Ocean Animals   Shapes   Sports**.

(1)	(2)	(3)
____	____	____
whale	baseball	pilot
shrimp	football	niece
shark	tennis	pastor

Exercise 6: In each column, cross out the one idea that does not support the underlined topic.

(1) **Vegetables**	(2) **Months**	(3) **Insects**
beans	December	wasp
finger	April	mosquito
corn	October	butter
potato	Jacob	ant

Exercise 7: In your journal, write a paragraph summarizing what you have learned this week.

Chapter 21 Test

Exercise 1: Classify each sentence. Use **SN** for subject noun, **V** for verb, **Adv** for adverb, **Adj** for adjective, **A** for article adjective, **P** for preposition, and **OP** for object of the preposition. For Sentence 2, underline the complete subject <u>one</u> time and the complete predicate <u>two</u> times.

1.   The   beautiful   butterfly   flew   quickly   away.

2.   The   fireman   climbed   carefully   to   the   roof.

Exercise 2: Underline the <u>syn</u> if the words are synonyms. Underline the <u>ant</u> if the words are antonyms.

1. below, beneath	syn ant	2. sweet, sour	syn ant	3. aid, help	syn ant

Exercise 3: Name the five parts of speech that you have studied. (*You may use abbreviations.*)

1. _____   2. _____   3. _____   4. _____   5. _____

Exercise 4: Match each subject part with the correct predicate part by writing the correct sentence number in the blank.

1. The player   _____ climbed in the trees.
2. The fire   _____ hatched today.
3. The tiny egg   _____ threw the ball.
4. Three monkeys   _____ baked in the oven.
5. An apple pie   _____ burned brightly.

Exercise 5: Write **S** for a complete sentence and **F** for a sentence fragment on the line beside each group of words below.

_____ 1. The ants marched across the ground.   _____ 6. The pain in his right hand.

_____ 2. To the man in the car.   _____ 7. Paid for the ticket with cash.

_____ 3. Many workers ride the subway.   _____ 8. At the bottom of the closet.

_____ 4. That new building.   _____ 9. Telephone rang.

_____ 5. Walter made several friends on the bus.

Exercise 6: In your journal, write a paragraph summarizing what you have learned this week.

Chapter 22 Test

Exercise 1: Classify each sentence. Use **SN** for subject noun, **V** for verb, **Adv** for adverb, **Adj** for adjective, **A** for article adjective, **P** for preposition, and **OP** for object of the preposition. For Sentence 1, underline the complete subject <u>one</u> time and the complete predicate <u>two</u> times.

1.   The   pretty   birthday   candles   melted   slowly   on   the   cake.

2.   The   excited   children   ran   to   the   pool.

Exercise 2: Underline the <u>syn</u> if the words are synonyms. Underline the <u>ant</u> if the words are antonyms.

| 1. night, day | **syn   ant** | 2. bashful, shy | **syn   ant** | 3. shout, whisper | **syn   ant** |

Exercise 3: Name the five parts of speech that you have studied. (*You may use abbreviations.*)

1. _____   2. _____   3. _____   4. _____   5. _____

Exercise 4: Correct the capitalization mistakes and put the rule number above each correction. Use the rule numbers in Reference 11 on page 17 in the Reference Section of your book. Put a (**.**) or a (**?**) at the end of the sentence.

_____(capitalization rule numbers)

our   church   meets   every   sunday   night   in   september ____ (3 capitals)

Exercise 5: Write the correct contraction in each blank. Use the contraction references to help you.

1. do not   _____

2. cannot   _____

3. I am   _____

4. are not   _____

5. were not   _____

Exercise 6: Write the correct words beside each contraction. Use the contraction references to help you.

1. didn't   _____

2. wasn't   _____

3. doesn't   _____

4. isn't   _____

5. I'm   _____

Exercise 7: In your journal, write a paragraph summarizing what you have learned this week.

Chapter 23 Test

Exercise 1: Classify each sentence. Use **SN** for subject noun, **V** for verb, **Adv** for adverb, **Adj** for adjective, **A** for article adjective, **P** for preposition, and **OP** for object of the preposition. For Sentence 2, underline the complete subject <u>one</u> time and the complete predicate <u>two</u> times.

1.   The   family   ate   cheerfully   in   the   kitchen   tonight.

2.   Tim   drove   quickly   to   school.

Exercise 2: Underline the <u>syn</u> if the words are synonyms. Underline the <u>ant</u> if the words are antonyms.

1. calm, quiet	syn ant	2. ask, tell	syn ant	3. sell, buy	syn ant

---

Exercise 3: Name the five parts of speech that you have studied. (*You may use abbreviations.*)

1. _____   2. _____   3. _____   4. _____   5. _____

Exercise 4: Identify the tense of each underlined verb by writing a number **1** for past tense, a number **2** for present tense, or a number **3** for future tense.

Verb Tense	Regular Verbs	Verb Tense	Irregular Verbs
	1. The girls <u>skipped</u> down the street.		7. Mom <u>gives</u> me a big hug.
	2. The girls <u>will skip</u> down the street.		8. Mom <u>will give</u> me a big hug.
	3. The girls <u>skip</u> down the street.		9. Mom <u>gave</u> me a big hug.
	4. Janet <u>works</u> at the bank.		10. The wind <u>blew</u> against the window.
	5. Janet <u>will work</u> at the bank.		11. The wind <u>will blow</u> against the window.
	6. Janet <u>worked</u> at the bank.		12. The wind <u>blows</u> against the window.

Exercise 5: Write the correct contraction in each blank. Use the contraction references to help you.

1. do not   _____

2. cannot   _____

3. I am   _____

4. are not   _____

5. were not   _____

Exercise 6: Write the correct words beside each contraction. Use the contraction references to help you.

1. didn't   _____

2. wasn't   _____

3. doesn't   _____

4. isn't   _____

5. I'm   _____

Exercise 7: In your journal, write a paragraph summarizing what you have learned this week.

Level 1 Homeschool Student Book

Chapter 24 Test

Exercise 1: Classify each sentence. Use **SN** for subject noun, **V** for verb, **Adv** for adverb, **Adj** for adjective, **A** for article adjective, **P** for preposition, and **OP** for object of the preposition. For Sentence 2, underline the complete subject <u>one</u> time and the complete predicate <u>two</u> times.

1. The   bouncy   little   puppies   barked   loudly   in   the   store.

2. Grandmother   laughed   at   the   grandchildren.

Exercise 2: Underline the <u>syn</u> if the words are synonyms. Underline the <u>ant</u> if the words are antonyms.

1. wild, tame	**syn ant**	2. push, shove	**syn ant**	3. add, subtract	**syn ant**

Exercise 3: Name the five parts of speech that you have studied. (*You may use abbreviations.*)

1. _____ 2. _____ 3. _____ 4. _____ 5. _____

Exercise 4: Identify the tense of each underlined verb by writing a number **1** for past tense, a number **2** for present tense, or a number **3** for future tense.

Verb Tense	Regular Verbs	Verb Tense	Irregular Verbs
	1. The cars <u>will race</u> around the track.		4. My flowers <u>grow</u> in the spring.
	2. The cars <u>raced</u> around the track.		5. My flowers <u>will grow</u> in the spring.
	3. The cars <u>race</u> around the track.		6. My flowers <u>grew</u> in the spring.

Exercise 5: Write the correct contraction in each blank. Use the contraction references to help you.

1. do not _____

2. cannot _____

3. I am _____

4. are not _____

5. were not _____

Exercise 6: Write the correct words beside each contraction. Use the contraction references to help you.

1. didn't _____

2. wasn't _____

3. doesn't _____

4. isn't _____

5. I'm _____

Exercise 7: On notebook paper, write a friendly letter to a friend or relative. Use References 27 and 28 as a guide to make sure your letter is in the correct friendly-letter format. Have your parents help you address an envelope. Mail your letter and wait for a response.

Exercise 8: In your journal, write a paragraph summarizing what you have learned this week.

Chapter 25 Test

Exercise 1: Classify each sentence. Use **SN** for subject noun, **V** for verb, **Adv** for adverb, **Adj** for adjective, **A** for article adjective, **P** for preposition, and **OP** for object of the preposition. For Sentence 1, underline the complete subject <u>one</u> time and the complete predicate <u>two</u> times.

1.   The   tiny   beetle   crawled   carefully   across   the   rocks.

2.   The   white   snow   melted   quickly.

Exercise 2: Underline the **<u>syn</u>** if the words are synonyms. Underline the **<u>ant</u>** if the words are antonyms.

1. round, square	**syn ant**	2. pull, tug	**syn ant**	3. bright, dim	**syn ant**

Exercise 3: Name the five parts of speech that you have studied. (*You may use abbreviations.*)

1. _____   2. _____   3. _____   4. _____   5. _____

Exercise 4: Write the correct contraction in each blank. Use the contraction references to help you.

1. do not _____

2. cannot _____

3. I am _____

4. are not _____

5. were not _____

Exercise 5: Write the correct words beside each contraction. Use the contraction references to help you.

1. didn't _____

2. wasn't _____

3. doesn't _____

4. isn't _____

5. I'm _____

Exercise 6: First, think of a person who has done something nice for you or has given you a gift (even the gift of time). On notebook paper, write a thank-you note to that person. Use the information in Reference 29 or 30 as a guide. Have your parents help you address an envelope. Mail your thank-you note.

Exercise 7: In your journal, write a paragraph summarizing what you have learned this week.

Chapter 26 Test

Exercise 1: Classify each sentence. Use **SN** for subject noun, **V** for verb, **Adv** for adverb, **Adj** for adjective, **A** for article adjective, **P** for preposition, and **OP** for object of the preposition. For Sentence 1, underline the complete subject <u>one</u> time and the complete predicate <u>two</u> times.

1. The   cute   little   rabbits   hopped   quickly   away.

2. Several   young   children   played   happily   in   the   park.

Exercise 2: Write the letters in each group below in alphabetical order.

1. k d r n   _____

2. h a s m o u   _____

Exercise 3: Put each group of words in alphabetical order. Use numbers to show the order in each column.

Zoo Words	Color Words	"B" Words
_____ 1. giraffe	_____ 5. yellow	_____ 9. brothers
_____ 2. monkey	_____ 6. green	_____ 10. buzzed
_____ 3. elephant	_____ 7. pink	_____ 11. beavers
_____ 4. tiger	_____ 8. red	_____ 12. balloon

Exercise 4: Put each group of words in alphabetical order. Use numbers to show the order in each column.

Food Words	"C" Words	Tree Words
_____ 1. taco	_____ 6. clowns	_____ 11. oak
_____ 2. hamburger	_____ 7. crib	_____ 12. maple
_____ 3. pizza	_____ 8. cute	_____ 13. walnut
_____ 4. hotdogs	_____ 9. church	_____ 14. cedar
_____ 5. steak	_____ 10. cats	_____ 15. pine

Exercise 5: In your journal, write a paragraph summarizing what you have learned this week.

Chapter 27 Test

Exercise 1: Classify each sentence. Use **SN** for subject noun, **V** for verb, **Adv** for adverb, **Adj** for adjective, **A** for article adjective, **P** for preposition, and **OP** for object of the preposition. For Sentence 1, underline the complete subject <u>one</u> time and the complete predicate <u>two</u> times.

1. The   funny   frog   hopped   in   the   water.

2. The   three   pretty   lamps   burned   brightly   today.

Exercise 2: Name the five parts of speech that you have studied. (*You may use abbreviations.*)

1. _____ 2. _____ 3. _____ 4. _____ 5. _____

Exercise 3: Write the correct contraction in each blank. Use the contraction references to help you.

1. do not _____
2. cannot _____
3. I am _____
4. are not _____
5. were not _____

Exercise 4: Write the correct words beside each contraction. Use the contraction references to help you.

1. didn't _____
2. wasn't _____
3. doesn't _____
4. isn't _____
5. I'm _____

Exercise 5: Underline the correct answer in each sentence.

1. Fiction books contain information and stories that are **(true, not true)**.
2. Nonfiction books contain information and stories that are **(true, not true)**.
3. The most common reference books are the dictionary and the encyclopedia. **(true, not true)**

Exercise 6: Put each group of words in alphabetical order. Use numbers to show the order in each column.

Number Words	Adverb Words	Proper Noun Words
_____ 1. two	_____ 5. carefully	_____ 9. Dan
_____ 2. three	_____ 6. away	_____ 10. Anna
_____ 3. four	_____ 7. today	_____ 11. Tim
_____ 4. five	_____ 8. suddenly	_____ 12. Sam

Exercise 7: In your journal, write a paragraph summarizing what you have learned this week.

ACTIVITY

SECTION

ACTIVITY / ASSIGNMENT TIME

Chapter 1, Lesson 4, Activity: Use one sheet of brown construction paper, one sheet of white construction paper, and one sheet of blue construction paper. Follow the directions given below to create different transportation groups.

1. On the brown sheet of paper, draw pictures of roads, trees, and flowers. Then, using newspapers, magazines, catalogs, etc., cut and paste several examples of ground transportation. (Examples: cars, trucks, vans, bicycles, motorcycles)

2. On the white sheet of paper, draw a sun, clouds, and birds. Then, cut and paste several examples of air transportation. (Examples: airplanes, helicopters, blimps, hot-air balloons)

3. On the blue sheet of paper, draw ocean waves and fish. Then, cut and paste several examples of water transportation. (Examples: motor boats, sail boats, cruise ships, jet skis, barges, submarines)

Chapter 2, Lesson 2, Activity: In the Word Search Puzzle below, find the following words and color each one a different color. The words will appear "down" or "across" in the puzzle.

ANIMALS		PEOPLE		PLACES		TOYS
T	P	L	A	C	E	S
P	Q	A	U	S	K	B
E	W	N	I	D	L	N
O	E	I	O	F	Z	T
P	R	M	P	G	X	O
L	T	A	A	H	C	Y
E	Y	L	B	O	Y	S
S	D	S	F	P	L	E

Chapter 2, Lesson 4, Activity: Choose four pieces of different-colored construction paper. Follow the directions given below to create different animal groups.

1. On the first piece of paper, write the title **Farm Animals**.

2. On the second piece of paper, write the title **Animal Pets**.

3. On the third piece of paper, write the title **Zoo Animals**.

4. On the fourth piece of paper, write the title **Jungle Animals**.

5. Search through old magazines, catalogs, newspapers, and books for examples of animals that would fit under each animal title.

6. Cut out and paste pictures of the animals on the appropriate pieces of construction paper. You may want to draw a few animals of your own.

Chapter 3, Lesson 4, Activity 2: In the Word Search Puzzle below, find the following words and color each one a different color. The words will appear "down" or "across" in the puzzle.

		HEAR	SIGHT	SMELL	TASTE	TOUCH	
S	M	E	L	L	A	S
U	E	Q	I	E	E	T
S	L	T	G	H	H	O
I	L	A	H	E	M	U
G	T	S	C	A	B	C
H	O	T	K	R	G	H
T	W	E	S	T	E	K

Chapter 4, Lesson 5, Activity: Write the correct numbers in the blanks to match the seasons with their activities. On writing paper, write a story about one of the seasons below.

_____Spring   _____Winter   _____Autumn   _____Summer

1   2   3   4

Chapter 5, Lesson 5, Activity 2: Help sing the Noun Soup Chant listed below.

Mmmm, hot, delicious noun soup. I am making noun soup. I need nouns for my soup. Won't you add a noun to my soup? This is hot, delicious noun soup. Please add a noun to my soup. Ahhh, yummy, yummy noun soup. It makes the tummy, tummy glad for noun soup. Mmmm, hot, delicious noun soup.

Thank you for helping with my noun soup. We are having fun making hot, delicious noun soup. Look at the nouns, swirling around, in our noun soup! Ahhh, noun soup, hot delicious noun soup.

Chapter 6, Lesson 3, Activity: Find all the nouns in the boxes below. Then, color each noun box yellow.

girls	ran	cats
sat	bears	walked
boys	played	dogs

Chapter 6, Lesson 4, Activity: Find all the verbs in the boxes below. Then, color each verb box red.

walked	played	cats
girls	ran	sat
boys	airplane	flew

Chapter 7, Lesson 3, Activity: Find all the synonyms words in the boxes below and color them orange. Then, find the antonym words and color them green.

sit, stand	lost, found	leap, jump
boat, ship	start, begin	empty, full
easy, hard	small, little	sad, happy

Chapter 7, Lesson 5, Activity: In the Word Search Puzzle below, find the following words and color each one a different color. The words will appear "down" or "across" in the puzzle.

ADVERB   ANTONYM   NOUN   SYNONYM   VERB

S	Y	N	O	N	Y	M
A	V	S	A	C	Q	W
A	N	T	O	N	Y	M
N	T	H	K	O	P	N
R	V	E	R	B	S	O
F	G	H	J	L	K	U
A	D	V	E	R	B	N

Chapter 9, Lesson 3, Activity: Follow the directions below to make a noun box.

Cover a shoe box and the lid of the shoe box with white paper. You can use glue or tape to make the white paper fit the box neatly. This is your noun box. Divide the inside of the shoe box into three sections with two cardboard pieces. Identify each section as **person, place,** or **thing**. Using items around the house *(magazines, catalogs, books, travel brochures, etc.),* cut out pictures of nouns and place them in their appropriate section.

Each night, have a member of the family draw a noun from the box. The family member must use the noun in a sentence that he/she writes on a strip of paper. After you read their sentence, color the sentence strip and glue it on the noun box. Friends and other relatives may also participate in decorating the noun box with sentence strips. They should sign their names on the sentence strips they have written. Later, another game can be played to guess who wrote the sentences using the nouns from the noun box. Everyone can guess who wrote the most sentences.

Chapter 10, Lesson 4, Activity: Use the code in the box below to find grammar words. Using the code numbers, write the correct letters for each blank. Then, make up your own code for several words.

Code		Words
1. n	7. j	n o u n a d v e r b
2. d	8. r	1 6 5 1 3 2 4 9 8 10
3. a	9. e	
4. v	10. b	v e r b a d j e c t i v e
5. u	11. t	4 9 8 10 3 2 7 9 13 11 12 4 9
6. o	12. i	
	13. c	

Chapter 11, Lesson 4, Activity: Using the scrambled letters below, circle every other letter, beginning with the first letter. Use the blank to write the new word created by writing each circled letter in order. (**spatikd**=said) On the title lines, write the title that best describes the words in each column. Choose from these titles: **Places**   **People**   **Airplanes**   **Animals**

Title:

c d h o i r l s d e r b e f n:

t h e u a n c y h u e w r h:

s r i m n p g w e c r g:

Title:

p s a m r a k z:

f n a o r f m e:

l g i h b m r c a d r k y:

Chapter 12, Lesson 2, Activity: Follow the directions below to make "A – An" Fruit Trees. Use these fruits for the activity:

apple   **apricot**   **cherry**   **coconut**   **lemon**   **orange**   **pear**   **plum**

Take two large paper bags and draw a giant round (circle) tree with a trunk on each sack. Next, put a large "A" on the top of one tree and a large "An" on the top of the second tree. Then, draw a circle on the appropriate tree for each fruit listed above and write the name of each fruit inside the circle. Color the tree green, the trunk brown, and each circle of fruit a different color.

Finally, go through the house finding five items that begin with a consonant sound to put in the "A" sack and five items that begin with a vowel sound to put in the "An" sack. Then, empty all the items into one big pile. The teacher will time you as you sort each item into the correct bag.

You can do this activity with others in the family. Have other family members put several different items in the sacks and empty the items into a big pile. You can time family and friends as they sort the items into the correct bags.

Chapter 13, Lesson 2, Activity: Find all the prepositions in the boxes below. Then, color each preposition box purple.

to	cats	in
jets	on	sat

Chapter 14, Lesson 2, Activity: Write the correct prepositions in the blanks. Use these prepositions:

across   at   by   down   in   on   to

Jack was a little brown squirrel that lived _____ a big oak tree. Jack wanted a new adventure. He sat _____ his tree and looked directly _____ the road. That's it! He would go _____ a trip. He would go all the way _____ the road. Then, he would run back _____ his tree.

First, he looked around. The coast was clear. Jack scampered _____ the tree _____ the ground. Next, he ran _____ the yard _____ a big tree _____ the road. He looked around again. Nothing. He took a deep breath and darted _____ the road. There! He had done it! He had gone _____ the road! Wow!

Suddenly, Jack was worried. He heard a sound. Jack was frightened! He ran wildly _____ the road. Then, he dashed back _____ the road. His heart was pounding _____ his chest! He finally got back _____ his tree. He jumped _____ a limb. Then, he climbed rapidly _____ his house. Jack was finally _____ his house. Then, he heard the sound again. Jack took no more chances. He sat contentedly _____ the window and never wanted another adventure.

Chapter 15, Lesson 3, Activity: Use the code in the box below to find <u>transportation</u> words. Using the code numbers, write the correct letters for each blank. Then, make up your own code for several words.

Code		Words
1. g	10. h	
2. t	11. p	<u>3</u> <u>10</u> <u>9</u> <u>11</u> <u>15</u> <u>9</u> <u>6</u> <u>16</u> <u>6</u> <u>13</u> <u>5</u>
3. s	12. x	
4. a	13. l	<u>2</u> <u>4</u> <u>12</u> <u>9</u> <u>2</u> <u>8</u> <u>4</u> <u>6</u> <u>2</u> <u>7</u> <u>8</u>
5. e	14. d	
6. c	15. b	
7. o	16. y	<u>3</u> <u>13</u> <u>5</u> <u>14</u> <u>2</u> <u>18</u> <u>1</u> <u>15</u> <u>7</u> <u>4</u> <u>2</u>
8. r	17. n	
9. i	18. u	<u>6</u> <u>4</u> <u>8</u> <u>3</u> <u>2</u> <u>8</u> <u>4</u> <u>9</u> <u>17</u> <u>3</u>

Chapter 16, Lesson 3, Activity: In the Word Search Puzzle below, find the following adjective words. The words will appear "down" or "across" in the puzzle. Color the adjectives going down blue and the adjectives going across yellow.

BEAUTIFUL	BOUNCY	CLEVER	CUTE	EARLY	GIANT
HUGE	ORANGE	STRONG	THICK	WEARY	YOUNG

S	W	E	A	R	L	Y	H	T	C
T	E	A	U	T	I	F	U	H	U
R	A	Y	O	U	N	G	G	I	T
O	R	A	W	O	K	D	E	C	E
N	Y	O	U	N	G	E	Z	K	B
G	O	S	G	I	A	N	T	U	O
E	C	L	E	V	E	R	O	H	U
H	S	O	R	A	N	G	E	I	N
B	E	A	U	T	I	F	U	L	C
Z	D	U	H	T	E	W	D	K	Y

Chapter 16, Lesson 4, Activity: In the Word Search Puzzle below, find the following preposition words and color each one a different color. The words will appear "down" or "across" in the puzzle.

ACROSS	AT	BY	DOWN	IN	ON	TO
A	T	A	B	I	N	E
Y	A	O	N	E	F	D
A	C	R	O	S	S	O
K	O	G	W	H	R	W
B	Y	M	N	T	O	N

Chapter 17, Lesson 4, Activity: In the Word Search Puzzle below, find the following adverb words and color each one a different color. The words will appear "down" or "across" in the puzzle.

HAPPILY	KINDLY	LOUDLY	RAPIDLY	SILENTLY	SLOWLY	TODAY	WARMLY
S	K	W	A	R	M	L	Y
I	N	L	J	M	C	E	R
L	K	I	N	D	L	Y	A
E	L	O	U	D	L	Y	P
N	B	D	F	H	S	W	I
T	U	T	O	D	A	Y	D
L	S	L	O	W	L	Y	L
Y	Q	W	E	R	T	U	Y
S	H	A	P	P	I	L	Y

Chapter 19, Lesson 3, Activity: Use the code in the box below to find <u>animal</u> words. Using the code numbers, write the correct letters for each blank. Then, make up your own code for several words.

Code		Words
1. w	10. r	
2. b	11. m	
3. e	12. f	
4. o	13. d	
5. i	14. g	
6. n	15. c	
7. l	16. u	
8. t	17. a	
9. s	18. h	
	19. k	

___ ___ ___ ___   ___ ___ ___ ___ ___ ___
1   4   7   12   15 17 11   3   7   9

___ ___ ___ ___   ___ ___ ___ ___ ___ ___ ___
14   4 17 8   8 16 10 8   7   3   9

___ ___ ___ ___   ___ ___ ___ ___ ___ ___ ___
2   5 10 13   15 18   5 15 19   3   6

Chapter 20, Lesson 5, Activity: In the Word Search Puzzle below, find the following vocabulary words and color each word a color of your choice. All the words begin with the letter *P*. The words will appear "down" or "across."

PARADE	PARK	PASSENGER	PATH	PIG	PINK	PLAYED	PONY	POOL
POOR	POPCORN	PORCH	PRETTY	PROUDLY	PUMPKINS	PUPPIES	PURPLE	

P	U	R	P	L	E	P	I	N	K
P	P	X	P	L	P	P	O	N	Y
A	A	P	R	U	O	P	O	O	L
R	S	U	E	M	R	X	P	Z	X
K	S	M	T	Q	C	S	R	P	P
P	E	P	T	A	H	Z	O	A	O
L	N	K	Y	P	I	G	U	R	P
A	G	I	X	C	X	A	D	A	C
Y	E	N	P	A	T	H	L	D	O
E	R	S	P	O	O	R	Y	E	R
D	P	U	P	P	I	E	S	C	N

Chapter 23, Lesson 5, Activity: Using the scrambled letters below, circle every other letter, beginning with the first letter. Use the blank to write the new word created by writing each circled letter in order. (**wpicnkd**=wind) On the title lines, write the title that best describes the words in each column. Choose from these titles: **Science**   **Clothes**   **Animals**   **Verbs**

Title:

r o a y i u n x c t o r a h t:

j h a u c n k y e u t w:

s r o m c p k w s c:

Title:

w s a m l a k b e r d:

s n h o o f u e t w:

s g m h i m l c e d d:

Chapter 26, Lesson 4, Activity: Using the scrambled letters below, circle every other letter, beginning with the first letter. Use the blank to write the new word created by writing each circled letter in order. (**npicnke**=nine) On the title lines, write the title that best describes the words in each column. Choose from these titles: **Colors**   **Weather**   **Shapes**   **Animals**

Title:

t m r y i u a x n o g r l h e:

r n e u c g t y a d n w g p l c e h:

s a q m u p a w r c e w:

Title:

w s i m n a d b y r:

c n l k o a u e d w y:

s g u h n m n c y d: